To:

Squirrel

Believe!

God's Graffiti Devotional:
From Prayers to Purpose

Crowdscribed
2575 Kelley Point Parkway, Suite 360, Edmond, OK 73013

Published in the United States by CrowdScribed, LLC

First published 2015
Library of Congress Cataloging-in-Publication Data
Library of Congress Control Number: 2015949917

Typeset by CrowdScribed in conjunction with Lightning Source, La Vergne, Tennessee

Printed in the United States by Lightning Source on acid-free paper.

Set in Universe LT Std
Book design by Brianna Spayd
Editor Cornelia Seigneur

ISBN 978-0-9905917-9-5

GOD'S GRAFFITI

-DEVOTIONAL-

FROM PRAYERS TO PURPOSE

CONTENTS

CONTRIBUTORS

KEVIN ALTON

is a youth and family ministry writer, author, and speaker. He's the co-creator of the Wesleyan youth resource Youthworker Circuit, senior writer and editor for the Wesleyan youth ministry community Youthworker Movement, and executive editor of the independent source of news and commentary United Methodist Reporter. Kevin lives in the Georgia woods outside of Chattanooga, TN, with his wife Britta and their two sons, Grey & Penner.

SHAWN CASSELBERRY

is a passionate advocate for God's justice, author of *God is in the City: Encounters of Grace and Transformation*, and Executive Director for Mission Year, a leading national Christian ministry that invites 18-29 year olds to pursue a lifestyle of loving God and loving people in the city (www.missionyear.org). Shawn has a passion for mentoring young adults and mobilizing the church around issues of racial and economic justice. As an ordained minister, Shawn speaks all across the country at colleges, churches, and conferences calling people to love God and love their neighbors. Shawn has been married to his wife Jen for 14 years and lives in the North Lawndale neighborhood on Chicago's west side. You can follow Shawn on Twitter: @Scasselberry

KATHY KHANG

is a regional multiethnic director for InterVarsity Christian Fellowship/USA, overseeing multiethnic training and ministry development in IL and IN. She blogs at www.morethanservingtea.wordpress.com and partners with other bloggers, pastors, and Christian leaders to highlight and move the conversation forward on issues of race, ethnicity, and gender within the Church. Kathy and her family live in the north suburbs of Chicago.

SANDRA MARIA VAN OPSTAL,

a second-generation Latina, is an author, speaker, and urban pastor who is passionate about creating spaces where voices from different cultures can come together in peace and overcome division. In her fifteen years with InterVarsity Christian Fellowship, Sandra mobilized thousands of college students for God's mission of reconciliation and justice in the world. Sandra's influence has also reached many others through her leadership and preaching on topics such of justice, poverty, racism, racial identity, reconciliation, and global mission. Sandra is a contributor to the Small Group Leader's Handbook (IVP) and author of The Mission of Worship (IVP). Her new book on multiethnic worship will be released Fall 2015. In addition to her national speaking, training, and writing, she serves as the Associate Pastor of Grace and Peace Community Church in Chicago. She can be followed on twitter at @sandravanopstal

ROMAL TUNE

is the embodiment of living beyond the label. After overcoming the setbacks of his upbringing and the destructive choices of his youth, he is now a sought-out communicator, community strategist, and education consultant. If it is true that a story must be lived before it is told, Romal's story of REDEMPTION is as genuine as it is moving. He is a cultivator of hope and dignity, moving individuals from setbacks to success.

CHAPTER ONE
- MOSES -

SHAWN CASSELBERRY

Day 1 - Moses Was Human

Sometimes I think about biblical characters like Moses and they seem larger than life. They are held up as lofty examples of strength and integrity that we cannot possibly reach. But that's because we know how the story ends. Think about it. We forget about Moses' humble beginnings and troubled past. We also overlook that Moses didn't know how his story would end while he was still living. He did not see himself as someone righteous and noble, someone who God could use. We forget that Moses was human, just like us. He had the same fears, anxieties, and insecurities. He probably had acne and had his heart broken like you and I have had. He undoubtedly had self-doubt, selfish tendencies, and sexual temptations. He had baggage. He had struggles. He was a person similar to you and me. The beauty of this story is not that God chose Moses because he was a perfect man, but that Moses was a very imperfect man, and regardless of this, God selected him. In fact, God *only* uses imperfect people because that's all God has to work with!

The amazing thing is that we have just as much potential to impact the world as Moses did. Romans 8:11 says, "The same spirit that raised Christ from the dead is living in you!" When we offer up our ordinary, imperfect lives for God to use, then we get empowered by an extraordinary, infinite power. The same God who called Moses from an ordinary human existence, also calls us to do great things. The question is: how will we respond?

Affirmation: The same spirit that was in Christ is in me.
Prayer: God, take my ordinary, imperfect human life and use me to do great things!

Day 2 - The Story of Your Life

Moses probably did not think his life would become a story that billions of people would end up reading about. After all, Moses had a rough start. He did not come from a great family. He was born into a Hebrew household at a time when Hebrews were enslaved and treated harshly

7

by the Egyptians in power. He almost died before he even had a chance to live. His mom sent him down the river in a basket to avoid being killed by Pharaoh, who was out to *slaughter* every Hebrew boy. But, then Moses was found and adopted by the daughter of the Pharaoh, and raised in a different culture. Moses later ended up killing an Egyptian for treating one of his fellow Hebrews harshly. When Moses' crime was discovered, he fled. Then, as God called Moses to free his people from slavery, Moses tried to run away. He came up with every excuse possible to not do what God was asking him to do. Though the beginning of Moses' story is turbulent, thankfully Moses allowed God to write the rest of his story. God was able to take a tragic life and turn it into a compelling narrative. Your life is a story, too, and God wants to help you write the ending. Who knows, perhaps God will use the chronicle of your life to inspire future generations, as he did with Moses.

Affirmation: My life is a story that needs to be written.
Prayer: God, help me write the ending of my story so that my life will inspire others.

Day 3 - Critical Choices

In life, we have defining moments when we have to make critical choices. These crossroads where we have to make important decisions could impact the rest of our lives. I am not talking about the small everyday decisions we make, like what we're going to order off the dollar menu. I'm talking about those moments when a lot is on the line. Choices like: will we stay in school? Will we avoid negative peer pressure? Will we go to college? Will we get married? Will we avoid compromising our principles for a quick buck? Will we stay on the path we feel God is leading us on, or will we take a short cut or a detour?

I have also experienced a few critical crossroads in my life, as I know you have as well. One of the biggest happened when I was a senior in high school. I was trying to decide where to go to college and what kind of life I wanted to pursue. I thought I had it figured out. I would go to a party school and major in business so I could earn lots of money. But then, during a church service I attended, I sensed God calling me to something more. In that moment, I was confronted with a major decision. I could choose a life focused on myself or choose a life devoted to a greater purpose. I had gone to church since I was in the womb and had asked Jesus into my heart, but that night I decided to commit my entire life to Him. I wanted the rest of my days to be spent serving others and making the world better for

8

all people. Moses too was confronted with a critical choice when he came to the burning bush (Exodus 3:2). Would he keep running from God and his past, or would he commit his life to something greater?

Affirmation: I have the power to make good choices.
Prayer: Lord, help me make wise choices so I can live my life with a greater purpose.

Day 4 - Stuck

Have you ever felt stuck in your life? Trapped in a bad relationship? Imprisoned in a dead-end job? Locked in a difficult situation? Aron Lee Ralston got physically stuck when a boulder fell on his arm while he was rock climbing in the mountains of Utah in 2003. His story was made into a movie in 2010 called *127 Hours*, and his part was played by the actor James Franco. After spending days trapped in the ravine, he realized he would die if he didn't find a way to get free. In an intense and disturbing moment of discernment, he cut his arm off to free himself from being stuck under the rock, and saved his own life in the process. This is an extreme example, but sometimes we can feel stuck in a similar way. We feel crushed by life circumstances and we do not feel like we have a way out. Many times we are trapped because there's an obstacle that's keeping us from being liberated. Sometimes there's a barrier that blocks our way to being all that we can be. Maybe it's negative influences, habits, or people who hold us back. Maybe it's our own pride or stubbornness. Jesus says in the book of Matthew, "If your right hand causes you to stumble (sin), cut it off and throw it away" (Matthew 5:30). Jesus does not mean for us to literally cut it off like Aron Ralston, but He does want us to get serious about removing the barriers that keep us from being the person God is calling us to be. What is the obstacle that is holding you back the most from being your most flourishing, prosperous self?

Affirmation: Nothing is going to hold me back from being the person I want to be.
Prayer: God, give me the courage to remove the obstacles that are standing in the way of me becoming the person you are calling me to be.

Day 5 - Abandonment

Being abandoned by the people you love is hard, no matter what the circumstances. Moses was abandoned by his mother in order for his

9

life to be saved, but I am sure that reality left a hole in Moses' heart. When people who are supposed to love and care for us leave us, it hurts. Growing up, I saw a lot of divorces occur that split families up and left my friends feeling abandoned. Now that I'm involved in urban ministry in Chicago, I see families split up by the prison system. I am involved in a ministry for youth with incarcerated loved ones. Many of them feel alone and abandoned while their relatives are in prison. We come alongside them to let them know they are not alone. They do not have to fear being discarded because for every fear we have, God has a promise. God's promise to us is this: "I will never leave you nor forsake you" (Hebrews 13:5). King David must have felt abandoned too because in Psalm 27 he says, "Though my father and my mother forsake me, the Lord will receive me." This gives us hope. No matter what we go through, God promises to be there. Even when our family can't be there for us, we can always rely on God to be there. God will never leave or forsake us.

Affirmation: I am not alone.
Prayer: When I feel alone or abandoned, help me Lord to remember your promise that You will never leave me nor forsake me.

Day 6 - Desperate Measures

Have you heard the expression, "Desperate times call for desperate measures?" When we end up in desperate situations we are willing to take extreme actions. Moses' mom was desperate. The Egyptian Pharaoh ordered that all Hebrew boys must be killed. These were desperate times. To save her son's life, she had to give him up. She became frantic, which required her to get creative. After finding a basket and lining it with tar to prevent water from getting in, she put Moses inside and placed it on the river where he was discovered by Pharaoh's daughter and thus spared from death. Sometimes we have to challenge the laws of our land to stand up for what's right. During the Holocaust, there were many who risked their lives to protect Jews from being killed by Hitler's army. They hid people, for example, in their attics in order to save lives. And, during the Civil Rights movement, people of all colors and creeds came together to stand against the laws that kept blacks from having equal rights as whites. We need to stand up and speak out whenever people are being oppressed.

We have to get creative. We have to do what we can to defend the vulnerable, just like Moses' mother did. Isaiah 1: 17 says, "Learn to do good; seek justice. Defend the oppressed. Take up the cause of the fatherless. Plead the case of the widow." There are many injustices in our world.

Hunger. Sickness and disease. Gun violence. Mass incarceration. Abuse. War. There are also many people in our communities who are in need and are being treated unfairly. What desperate measures are you willing to take to stand up for other people who are hurting?

Affirmation: I will stand up for what is right.
Prayer: God, help me to stand up against injustice and stand with those who are being oppressed.

Day 7 - Motivations and Methods

When Moses saw an Egyptian beating a Hebrew slave, he stepped in and killed the Egyptian. His motivation was to help his fellow man, but his method was violence and murder. Throughout our life we have to check our motivations and our methods. Our motivation is the reason we do the things we do. Are we motivated out of love, guilt, anger, fear, or defensiveness? Do I help someone else because I want something in return, or do I do it because I genuinely care about people? Once we check our motivation, we have to choose the right method. Moses had a good motivation to protect the slave from being brutally beaten, but he chose a method of violence that ended in murder. We can be right in motivation but wrong in method. Dr. Martin Luther King, Jr. displayed the right motivation and the right method during the Civil Rights movement. Despite violent opposition and death threats to himself and his family, Dr. King chose to respond in love. He was motivated by love and he chose a method of non-violence to respond to his enemies. Dr. King said, "Darkness cannot drive out darkness; only light can do that. Hate cannot drive out hate; only love can do that." Love has to be our motivation, while peace and non-violence has to be our method. Do you struggle more with having the right motivation or having the right method?

Affirmation: I am a loving and peaceful person.
Prayer: God, help me to have love as my motivation, and non-violence and peace as my methods.

Day 8 - Sacrifice Is Life

Nothing of worth is gained without sacrifice. If you want to be a star athlete it requires sacrifice and dedication. If you want to raise a family it will require your surrender of time, sleep, and money. If you want to graduate from college it will require some forfeit of your social life to spend time studying. This is how our world is set up. It is one of the principles of life. Sacrifice is life. The life of Moses is an example of this. The people of Israel could not be freed from slavery if Moses was not willing to give up his own plans for God's call. Christ showed us that the way to life is through sacrifice. There is no resurrection without a cross. However, a lot of us want to skip the sacrifice and acquire the reward. We want the fast money without the work. We want the resurrection without having to go through the cross. But there's no true, authentic life without sacrifice. The deep life, the abundant life of Christ, is the life of commitment. The depth of the sacrifice is the depth of the life you experience. The temptation will always be to avoid sacrifice. You will be tempted to take short cuts, to cheat, and to seek a life of comfort and ease. But this only keeps you from growing deeper and having a more meaningful life. Sacrifice is the path to a rewarding life. Sacrifice is life. "Therefore, I urge you, brothers and sisters, in view of God's mercy, to offer your bodies as a living sacrifice, holy, and pleasing to God—this is your true and proper worship" (Romans 12:1).

Affirmation: I can accomplish anything if I am willing to make the sacrifice.
Prayer: Lord, help me offer my life as a living sacrifice so that I can experience the depths of life.

Day 9 - Adoption

Did you know over 120,000 children are adopted each year in the United States? When someone is adopted it means they have been welcomed into a new family. They have been chosen, desired, and accepted. Moses was adopted by the daughter of Pharaoh. She could have had him killed or let him continue to float down river, but she had compassion for him. She decided to take him into her family and love him as her own. Adoption is a beautiful picture of what God has done for us. Galatians 4:4-6 says, "But when the right time came, God sent his Son, born of a woman, subject to the law. God sent him to buy freedom for us who were slaves to the law, so that He could adopt us as his very own children. And because we are his children, God has sent the Spirit of his Son into our hearts, prompting us to call out, 'Abba, Father.'" We have been adopted into God's family. All the rights and privileges Jesus has as a child of God, we now have. Adoption is a powerful symbol of God's love for us. Maybe you were adopted as a child or youth. Maybe you have considered adopting when you get older. I hope we all can see that being adopted, whether by a family or by God, is a special act that shows our great value.

Affirmation: I am loved and chosen by God.
Prayer: Thank you, Lord, for adopting me into your family and loving me as You love your son Jesus.

Day 10 - Navigating Cultures

Moses lived between two cultures. Moses was Hebrew by birth, but was adopted into an Egyptian family. As such, Moses was bi-cultural, and these cultures could not have been more different. The Hebrews were slaves, while the Egyptians were slave-masters. The Hebrews suffered under harsh treatment and the Egyptians lived a life of privilege. Moses found himself caught in between. In some ways, he related to being Hebrew. This is why he defended the Hebrew slave that was being beaten. In other ways, he related to being Egyptian. As the adopted son of Pharaoh's daughter, he enjoyed privileges other Hebrews did not receive. Moses had to figure out where he belonged. Similarly, we all navigate throughout different cultures. It can be hard to know which culture we belong to. But the cool thing is: God uses all of Moses' cultural experiences. Because Moses is a Hebrew he is able to relate to the struggling Hebrew people and then lead them, and because Moses grew up in Egyptian culture he is able to confront those in power to do the right thing. Our cultural background is no accident. God uses every aspect of our lives. Between what cultures do you navigate? What do you like about your cultural background? Do you see your own people struggling? How can you use your power and voice to bring freedom to others?

Affirmation: My cultural heritage is not an accident.
Prayer: God, help me navigate cultures so I can help those who are suffering and confront those in power to do what's right.

Day 11 - Does God Care?

Sometimes it can seem like God is not there or that God does not care about us. In Exodus 3:7, the Lord tells Moses, "I have indeed seen the misery of my people in Egypt. I have heard them crying out because of their slave drivers, and I am concerned about their suffering." God cares! God cares about those who suffer. God cares about us. God sees our struggles and hears our calls for help. In our hardest times and most painful moments, God is watching. God is not standing by waiting to cast judgment on us for our failures. He is a compassionate God who sees our misery and hears our cries. God even listens to the cries that we don't have the strength to utter. The Exodus story is a reminder that God is deeply concerned about humanity and willing to step into human history to help us. God cared so much about humanity that He stepped into human history again in the form of Jesus. On the cross, we find that God not only sees our misery and hears our cries, but He feels our pain. God does not stand at a distance. God comes close. The message of the cross is loud and clear: God cares.

Affirmation: God cares about me.
Prayer: I cast my cares on you, God, because I know you care for me.

Day 12 - God's Secret Weapon

"What's the game plan?" I bet that's what Moses was wondering. What does God do after seeing the misery and hearing the cries of the Hebrew people in Egypt? What is God's response to the suffering? I can imagine Moses thinking, "Oh snap, God is going to come down here and teach Pharaoh a lesson!" Moses had no idea what God's secret weapon would be. God tells Moses, "I have come down to rescue the people from the power of the Egyptians. . . so now go. I am sending you to bring my people, the Israelites, out of Egypt." Wait, what? God's secret weapon was Moses! God is a powerful God. God created the heavens and the earth. God could speak the word and Pharaoh's army would be destroyed. So why does God use Moses? God doesn't *need* Moses, but God chooses to use Moses. In this example, we see that God wants to work together with us to restore the world. God wants to develop us into leaders in the same way God developed Moses. You are God's secret weapon. God wants to use you to impact your school, church, and community. Do you see things that are not right? Are you waiting on God to act? Maybe God is waiting on you!

Affirmation: I am God's secret weapon.
Prayer: God, develop me as a leader like You developed Moses so I can impact the world.

Day 13 - Who Me?

Have you ever had someone believe in you more than you believed in yourself? Maybe it was a coach or teacher who saw potential in

you when you didn't see it in yourself. One time during PE class I was running around the track and the teacher asked to speak with me after class. He said, "Are you trying out for the track team?" I said, "No sir." He then raised his voice and said to me again, "Casselberry! Are you trying out for the track team?" I said, "Yes, sir." I tried out and made the team. I went on to run cross-country in college, I coached track and cross-country for a couple of years, and I continue to run in road races to this day. All this happened because my PE teacher saw something in me that I didn't see in myself. Likewise, God saw something in Moses that Moses didn't see in himself. God saw someone who could deliver his people out of Egypt. But Moses had a lot of self-doubt and insecurity. He responded to God, "Who am I that I should go?" Moses had a lot of reasons why God should pick someone else. But when God calls us to do something, God always equips us. God does not expect us to do it on our own. God reassured Moses, "I will be with you." Do you doubt your own talents? Do you wrestle with self-doubt? You have so much potential! You have gifts and talents God wants to use for greater purposes! When there's a need for a leader, step up. You may not feel ready, but God will prepare you as you go.

Affirmation: I am a gifted and talented person.
Prayer: God, equip me to be the leader you are calling me to be.

Day 14 - God Speaks Part I: Through Nature

I have never seen a burning bush. It would be great if God would just set the shrubs in front of my house on fire every time I needed to make a big decision. But God doesn't work like that. Do you know how many times God speaks to someone through a burning bush in the Bible? One time, to Moses. God does not speak with anyone else in the Bible through a burning bush. God does not even speak to Moses again through a bush. If you're expecting God to speak to you through a burning bush, it is not likely to happen. But that does not mean that God is not trying to get your attention. God is speaking to us all the time, but most of the time we don't notice. God uses all kinds of ways to get our attention. One way God speaks to us is through nature. Have you ever been in awe at a sunset across a city skyline? Have you ever felt peace standing on the beach listening to the roar of the waves? Like an artist communicates through his or her artwork, God communicates to us through the created world. Look around today as you go to school or work. Notice the trees, the flowers, the sky, the wind, and the animals you encounter. St. Theophan the Recluse said, "All things in creation witness to the Father." Do you hear God speaking to you through nature? What does nature tell you about God?

Affirmation: I can encounter God through nature.
Prayer: Lord, speak to me through the world you have created.

Day 15 - God Speaks Part II: Through Scripture

Another way God speaks to us is through scripture. Has someone ever written you a love letter? Did you read it once and then throw it away? Probably not. You most likely read it over and over again. The Bible is God's love letter to humanity. It's by reading the Bible that we understand God's love for us. In Jeremiah 31:3, God says, "I have loved you with an everlasting love." And Zephaniah 3:17 says, "The Lord your God is in your midst. A victorious warrior. God will exult over you with joy, God will quiet you with love, God will rejoice over you with shouts of joy." I used to think that God was a judgmental God just waiting for me to mess up. I used to think God enjoyed sending people to Hell. Meditating on scriptures of God's love helped me to hear God's voice of love for me and for the rest of humanity. Now I can say with Paul, "I am convinced that neither death, nor life, nor angels, nor demons, nor principalities, nor things present, nor things to come, nor powers, nor height, nor depth, nor any other created thing, will be able to separate us from the love of God in Christ Jesus (Romans 8:38)." God wants to speak to us through the scriptures. If you haven't heard God's voice speaking to you in a while, it might be time to re-read some of those old love letters.

Affirmation: I am loved with an everlasting love.
Prayer: Speak to me through your Word, God.

Day 16 - God Speaks Part III: Through People

God speaks to us through other people. For some reason, God loves using people as a mouthpiece. God chooses Moses to be his voice to Pharaoh and the slaves in Egypt. God could have just spoken from the sky, but God likes including other people in sharing the message. God spoke to the nation of Israel through the prophets. They warned the people about idolatry and injustice. Idolatry is when we put someone or something above God. God knows that if we put our hopes in anyone else but God we will only end up disappointed and hurt. Injustice is when we mistreat or oppress people. The prophets reminded us that we cannot claim to love God if we don't stand up for the poor and vulnerable. God still speaks through people. God speaks through singers, poets,

preachers, and writers. God will speak through anyone who makes themselves available to share God's message of love and justice. Has God ever used someone to speak truth into your life? Maybe it was a pastor, mentor, or friend who gave you wise counsel at just the right moment. Has God used you to speak truth to someone else?

Affirmation: I can be used by God to communicate God's love and justice.
Prayer: Dear God, speak to me through your people. Speak through me to your people.

Day 17 - God Speaks Part IV: Through Silence

God also speaks through silence. God's voice is not always loud. 1 Kings 19:12 tells the story of how the prophet Elijah wanted to hear the voice of God. He listened for God in the earthquake, but God was not in the earthquake. After the earthquake, Elijah listened for God in the fire, but God was not in the fire. After the fire, there was a still small voice. It is in the still small voice that Elijah hears the message from God. Sometimes we can hear God's still small voice in silence and solitude. If we can unplug from all our technologies and turn off all the noise around us, we might be better able to hear God speaking to us from within. If you never listen for God, it will make it very hard for you to hear Him. Psalm 46:10 says, "Be still and know that I am God." This passage indicates we can know God deeply and intimately when we slow down and get still. Quiet your soul today. Take five or ten minutes to be still. You don't have to say any words. Just be still and know that God is God.

Affirmation: I can know God deeply and intimately.
Prayer: Lord, still my soul and commune with me.

Day 18 - Questioning God

In youth group, we tried to baffle our youth pastors by asking questions like, "Can God create a rock that He can't move?" If God could do anything, then God could make a rock impossible to move. But if God could make a rock that He couldn't move, then that means there's something God couldn't do. It was a fun way to question the faith I had been taught and put our youth pastor on the spot. As I got older, I had more questions about my faith that weren't a laughing matter. I questioned why there was evil in the world. I questioned if God was really concerned about justice for the poor. I questioned whether people who had never heard the gospel would really burn in Hell for eternity. I was afraid to ask these questions. I wasn't sure if I was allowed to question God. But in scripture, people like Moses and Abraham weren't afraid to question God. They knew God would not punish them for asking questions. Asking questions brought them to a deeper place of faith. God gave a promise to the prophet Jeremiah, "You will seek me and you will find me when you seek me with all your heart" (Jeremiah 29:13). Sometimes our faith is shallow because we are afraid of asking questions. Seeking answers to my questions led me to study scripture more fervently and to make my faith my own. Don't be afraid to seek the truth. That's how you find God.

Affirmation: When I seek truth I will find God.
Prayer: God, bring me to a deeper place of faith through my questions.

Day 19 - Crutches

In middle school, my cousin and I raced down a steep hill on skateboards. Once, I was going so fast that the skateboard started shaking violently about halfway down the hill. I knew I had to do something quickly or I would wipe out and be in serious trouble. I put my foot down on the ground to try to slow down but the board kept going and my ankle ended up twisting. I sprained my ankle, which required me to hobble around on crutches for weeks. Have you ever used crutches? Crutches help stabilize you so you can allow the place of pain the time and space to heal. Crutches are a support system for your physical body. Support systems are needed for emotional wounds too. We need people who can support us when we are going through tough sensitive times. Who is your support system? What areas of your life are in need of healing? Don't be afraid to share what you are going through with people in your life who care about you.

Affirmation: I have people around who care about me.
Prayer: God, help me to allow others to support me when I am hurting.

Day 20 - Counseling

I am a big fan of counseling. I have seen God work in the context of counseling more than in any other arena. When we deal with the past, we find greater freedom and healing. God can only heal what is brought to light. When we hide or bury our hurt, we cannot be restored and we cannot move forward. People often fight the idea of counseling at first. There is a stigma that counseling is only for people with severe mental problems. This is a lie that keeps people from receiving the healing they need. If our arm were severed, we would go to the hospital. We wouldn't think twice. When we are emotionally severed, we need to go to counseling. One of the words used in the Bible to describe the Holy Spirit is "counselor." I have experienced the Holy Spirit most noticeably in my life in the counseling context. Jesus said the Spirit would lead us into all truth. Counseling helps us to tell the truth, and the truth truly sets us free. By addressing the broken places in our heart, we see that God longs for our healing and leads us to truth and wholeness. As the late Henri Nouwen put it, we are "wounded healers." When we find healing for ourselves, we can help others experience healing too.

Affirmation: I am a wounded healer.
Prayer: Help me bring my wounds to light so You can heal them.

Day 21 - Saying "I'm S----."

Two of the hardest words to say are, "I'm sorry." It's so hard to admit mistakes. Why is that? Why can't we just say those two simple words? When you say you're sorry, it disarms the other person. When you acknowledge what you have done, it allows the other person to acknowledge their part. Most of the time, the situation becomes a standoff of who is right and who is wrong. No one wants to be the first to humble himself and admit any fault. But, I think it's actually a sign of strength to be the first one to say you're sorry. When you are able to admit you are not perfect, then the other person can admit he is not perfect. No one is perfect. Everyone will make mistakes and needs to say the words, "I am sorry." I think they are the most important words besides, "I love you." If you can learn to say them now, then your relationships will be much better in the future. Someone who can't say, "I'm sorry," will not have very many deep relationships. Forgiveness is something you need to give and receive. You can't receive forgiveness if you never say you're sorry. After 14 years of marriage, I have learned to say, "I'm sorry. I was wrong. Will you forgive me?" I think it's important to say those words as a leader, too. You are going to make mistakes in relationships and in leadership. Being a great leader is not about being perfect, but being able to say, "I'm sorry," when you've made a mistake.

Affirmation: It's a sign of strength to say, "I'm sorry."
Prayer: Lord, help me to be humble and admit my mistakes.

Day 22 - Real Men (and Women) Cry

I don't know where we get this bogus idea that real men don't cry. Why would God create emotions if we weren't supposed to feel them? Why do we have tear ducts? The shortest verse in scripture is, "Jesus wept." Jesus felt grief. Jesus showed emotion. Crying is a natural response to death, tragedy, grief, and sadness. Was Jesus a real man? I think Jesus was more of a man than anyone who has lived. I think Jesus was trying to teach us that it is ok to cry. Although Jesus was fully God, Jesus was trying to show us what it means to be fully human. Being fully human means embracing the full range of human emotions. If we cut off our feelings then we are denying part of our humanity. Maybe men do not like crying, but real men know how to share their emotions. They know how to show affection to their families. Maybe you have been taught that it's not okay to show emotions. Maybe you have learned to bottle up your feelings instead of expressing them in healthy ways. Or, maybe you are afraid of your emotions and what might happen if you let them out. Be honest about where you are, but don't say real men don't cry. It's just not true.

Affirmation: Real men and women cry.
Prayer: Jesus, help me express my emotions so I can be fully human.

Day 23 - Running from God

I grew up in the church as a pastor's kid. The last thing I envisioned for my life as an adult was serving in ministry. I knew I had ministry gifts and leadership abilities. I knew I wanted to live differently. I knew I wanted to live out my faith radically. But I still ran. Like Jonah, who ran from his calling, I wanted to go the other direction. I can relate to Moses who came up with every excuse why God should pick someone else to be his mouthpiece. Why do we run from God? Why do we hide like Adam and Eve did in the garden? God is a gracious God who has good plans for our lives. God doesn't want to steal our fun, but instead He wants us to discover our created purpose. When we stop running, we see that God is not someone to be feared. God is someone to be trusted. God wants to use you for great things. You do not have to be afraid. What has God been calling you to do that you have been running from? Maybe it's leading a bible study with your friends, or being a mentor to a younger kid, or going on a mission trip, or running for political office. Don't let fear hold you back from your destiny with God. It's time to stop running and it's time to start doing what God has put in your heart to do.

Affirmation: I will not let fear hold me back from my destiny.
Prayer: God give me boldness to pursue what you have put in my heart.

Day 24 - Running from Our Past

A mentor of mine shared a piece of wisdom his dad gave him when he was about to make a big decision in his life. His dad told him to make sure he is running toward something and not running from something. That is good advice. So often we make decisions because we want to run away from something rather than toward something. We run from bad family situations, bad relationships, negative peer influences, pain, failure, and hurt. We all find ourselves running from things at some point in our lives. When I graduated from high school, I left the state and never turned back. I wanted to leave my failures behind me and become an entirely new person. My desire for godliness and my actual experience did not line up. As a perfectionist, I struggled with embracing myself, my broken self, as dearly loved by God. In college, I had a revelation that God called me in my brokenness and weakness, not in my strength. Once I finally drank in this simple, yet hard to swallow truth, I did not have to run or hide anymore. God was calling me toward something greater than I could have imagined. God was not shocked at my failure or embarrassed by my weakness. In fact, God knew that I could not be what I wanted to be without the Holy Spirit. We all have experienced pain, heartbreak, and failure. Many of us are running from our past, perhaps something we have done or something done to us. I think about Moses, who killed an Egyptian and fled into the desert as a fugitive. God called Moses while he was on the run, then gave him something to run toward. God wants us running toward our purpose, our dreams, and our destiny; not from our pain, our past, or our disappointment.

Affirmation: I will run toward my purpose, not from my past.
Prayer: Lord, pour your love into my heart through your Holy Spirit.

Day 25 - Strength for Weakness

We are taught early on in life not to show weakness. We work hard to appear like we have it altogether. But God likes to use weakness to show off his glory. In 1 Corinthians 1:27, Paul says, "But God chose the weak things of the world to shame the strong." God does not choose to work through our strength but through our weakness. Paul said God's power is "made perfect in weakness" (2 Cor. 12:9). That's why Paul boasted in his weakness so God would get more glory. When we share our testimony about what we've been through, we are able to give credit to God, not ourselves. God gives us strength for weakness. If we pretend to be strong, acting as if we don't need God, then we can't receive the strength God offers us. It is when we are weak, broken, and humble, that God responds with strength, healing, and power. God offers us a sweet deal. Give God your weakness, and in return, God will give you strength.

Affirmation: When I am weak, then I am strong.
Prayer: Lord, I will take your strength for my weakness.

Day 26 - Moving

One of my worst childhood memories was moving. My dad had to move for a job and it meant leaving the place I called home. I had to leave my best friends and start all over somewhere new. My family thought I was handling it so well, but they did not know that I would cry alone in my room because I did not want to go. As a protest to the move, I lived out of my suitcase for the first six months in the new house. Moses also had to relocate after growing up his whole life in the palace in Egypt. Moving is scary because you are leaving everything that's familiar to go somewhere unknown. Moving requires you to make new friends, which can take time. If you have to move multiple times it can make it hard to open yourself up to other people. You are less likely to trust right away because you don't know how long you will be there. But moving did open my eyes to a larger world. I gained new perspectives and eventually new friends. Relocating gave me a spirit for adventure. I noticed there was more of the world to see. Now I travel a lot for work and for fun. I have been to Italy, India, England, Egypt, Argentina, Mexico and cities across our country. I love experiencing new places and new cultures. Have you had to move a lot? What was hard about moving? What turned out to be good?

Affirmation: I will look for the good in every situation.
Prayer: God, help me to voice my pain so I can grow into the person I am meant to be.

Day 27 - Leadership Lessons: Becoming a Leader

Moses started out as a reluctant leader, but ended up being very strong and capable in his role. Moses is a great example of what it takes to become a great leader. Becoming a leader requires (1) saying "yes" when God calls you to lead; (2) overcoming self-doubt and fear; (3) relying on God's strength, not your own; (4) having courage to continue when you face challenges; and (5) being patient with yourself and the people you lead. Moses could have ignored the call of God but he ended up saying yes. He overcame self-doubt and depended on God to have his back when facing Pharaoh. He was courageous when Pharaoh's heart was hardened; Moses did not back down. He had to learn patience with himself when he made mistakes and he had to have patience with the people he led who kept complaining. These same leadership lessons are necessary whether you are leading a sports team, church group, or business meeting. When leadership is required or asked of you, do not be afraid. Take the first step and say yes. The next steps are sure to follow from there.

Affirmation: I am becoming a leader.
Prayer: Dear God, take me from a reluctant leader to a strong and capable leader.

Day 28 - Leadership Lessons: Thermometer versus Thermostat

What kind of leader are you? Are you a thermometer or a thermostat? A thermometer just mimics the temperature in the room. Whatever the group thinks, a thermometer type of leader thinks the same thing. If the group is negative, the thermometer leader is negative too. On the other hand, a thermostat sets the temperature in the room. The thermostat changes the atmosphere of the room. If the group is negative, the thermostat leader sets a positive tone. The thermometer leader is a people pleaser. The thermostat leader is willing to "speak the truth in love" for the growth of the group. You can tell who the thermostat leaders are in every group. They do not give in to peer-pressure; they know who they are and they are willing to take a stand for what they believe; and they are people who become the change they want to see in the world. We need more thermostat leaders who can set a positive tone for others and lead by example. So I ask you again, which kind of leader are you?

Affirmation: I have the power to change the atmosphere in the room.
Prayer: Lord, may I become the kind of leader who can set an example that others will follow.

Day 29 - A Great Purpose

Moses could never have imagined the life he would live. God called him out of a past of shame and into a life of purpose. He did not let fear keep him from his destiny, nor did he not let Pharaoh's power cause him to cower. He was not perfect, but he made himself available to be used by

God. Now it's your turn. You can't even imagine what God has in store for you. Ephesians 3:20 states that God is "able to do immeasurably more than all we ask or imagine, according to the power working within us." God wants to work in your life beyond what you can even comprehend. First Corinthians 2:9 says, "No eye has seen, no ear has heard, no mind conceived, the things God has prepared for those who love Him." God loves to blow our minds. God takes the little we give and multiplies it. God gives strength for weakness. We settle for an average life, but God imagines an incredible life for us; we want to just forget about our past while God wants to redeem it; we want to have a good life, and God wants us to have an abundant life. You were created for a great purpose. Do not settle for anything less.

Affirmation: I will not settle for less than God's best.
Prayer: Lord, I want to experience all that you have for me.

Day 30 - Becoming Whole

Why did Jesus heal people? Why did Jesus give sight to the blind and heal lepers? Why did Jesus spend so much time addressing people's physical needs? Why didn't Jesus just come and preach sermons or give them steps to get to heaven? The reason is that healing is part of the nature of God. God is wholeness and we cannot be around God without experiencing healing. God does not just want us to believe in all the right things; he also wants to see our whole lives transformed. Jesus will not let us continue on our faith journey without us addressing what hurts us and working to become whole. None of us chose where we were born. Though the blind man Jesus heals in John 8 didn't do anything wrong to have his condition, Jesus' disciples presumed he was blind because he or his family had sinned. But, Jesus makes it clear that he did not choose to be blind. Jesus says, "Neither this man nor his family sinned, but this happened so that the works of God might be displayed." We start where we are, regardless of our choices. And, despite the setbacks in our lives, God is able to do mighty works in our lives. God desires for all of us to move from brokenness to wholeness. The past can't be changed but we can write a new script for the future. Healing comes when we let God work in us, especially in the deep places of pain. God won't force healing on us --- we have to choose it for ourselves. We have to open our hearts for God to come in and heal us.

Affirmation: God wants me to be whole.
Prayer: Lord, make me whole.

CHAPTER TWO

- RAHAB -

KATHY KHANG

Day 1 - Don't Assume

The minute we meet Rahab we know who she is and what she did. We immediately find out she is a prostitute. I don't know about you, but that is not how I would like to be known, especially if I was going to be mentioned in the Bible. I want to be known for the things that put me in a good light with other people because I know how I view other people. My tendency is to make a lot of assumptions and pass judgment on others before getting to know them, which makes it difficult to capture the full picture of a person and her situation. If we all did that in the situation of Rahab and the spies, imagine how that would limit the way we engaged with them. What would've happened if the spies, sent out by Joshua and the Lord, skipped over Rahab and her house because of her reputation? What would have happened if God skipped over us because of what we had done or who we have been in the past?

Affirmation: God doesn't skip over people because of their past.
Prayer: God, help me see others the way You look at them.

Day 2 - A Label Isn't a Limit

There are a lot of ways we are labeled and label each other. Sometimes we do it out of love and affection, such as when we are given a nickname, but in other situations, labels point out faults, weaknesses, or mistakes. My sister was called the "pretty one" and I was called the "smart one," which made her think she was stupid and made me think I was ugly. We let the labels limit us and make us see ourselves in limited ways. We know Rahab is a prostitute, not the kind of thing you want to be known for, and yet there she is. She doesn't let her label stop her from acting on her convictions and beliefs.

Affirmation: God doesn't limit you to a label.
Prayer: God, help us see ourselves for more than how others see us.

Day 3 - Hospitality Is a Choice

In our world, it's easy to think only of our own needs and comforts. Risk-taking is more often connected with bungee jumping or skydiving, and not necessarily with being open and welcoming toward others. But that is exactly what God invites us to do: risk our own needs and comforts to welcome others. Rahab chose to open her doors and welcome and hide the spies instead of kicking them out, which in my mind would have been the easier more comfortable (and safer!) way to go. I don't know how often I'm willing to welcome strangers into my conversations let alone into my home, but Rahab's example challenges all of us to consider being more hospitable.

Affirmation: It's not always comfortable or safe to obey God.
Prayer: God, help me be more welcoming and open to others even if it's uncomfortable.

Day 4 - Fear Doesn't Have to Stop You

The word was out. The God of Israel had split the Red Sea and created a dry path for His people to safely pass through. He was delivering His people, and they were headed for Jericho. The king of Jericho knew things were getting bad for his people, and he knew spies were around. The people of Jericho weren't safe. Rahab knew it too. "When we heard of it, our hearts melted in fear and everyone's courage failed, for the Lord your God is God in Heaven above and on the earth below." But Rahab didn't let her fear and failed courage stop her. She didn't give up, and she didn't turn in the spies because she could see past the fear of being destroyed; she saw hope for a future and put her faith not in the king, but in the God who was saving people.

Affirmation: Don't let fear stop you from seeing God for who He is.
Prayer: God, help me identify my fear so that I can make space for faith and hope.

Day 5 - Trust Is Risky

I imagine a prostitute has little reason to trust people, especially strange men, which is why I think Rahab was crazy to do what she did. Instead of obeying the authority of the king of Jericho to turn in the spies, she trusts the spies to spare her and her family's lives in return for hiding them. She doesn't even make the deal before hiding them. She takes the risk, hides the spies, lies to the king's men (I don't generally recommend lying), and then talks with the spies who now have control over the situation. They outnumber her. She knows their God is giving Jericho up to them. And yet she doesn't let that, or past disappointments, or past broken promises stop her. Rahab has many reasons to be a bitter, distrusting woman but she isn't.

Affirmation: Learning from your mistakes doesn't have to mean anger or distrust.
Prayer: Teach me to trust in You, God, even when people have broken trust in the past.

Day 6 - Teachers Come in All Shapes and Sizes

I'm fairly certain that if a prostitute walked into church and tried to teach Sunday school, there would be more than a few people raising their eyebrows. I'm not sure Rahab would have felt comfortable walking into a church nowadays. And there may be many days, months, or years that you or someone you know has felt like she could never walk into a church, let alone have anything to say about God. However, here Rahab is in the Bible to be an example to future generations, that believing in the presence and power of God is an incredible, risky, daring, and attractive option, even for a prostitute. God didn't "fix" her and then let her teach us through her story. He used her entire story.

Affirmation: God won't erase part of my story.
Prayer: Praise God who redeems our whole life!

Day 7 - What You Know Is Important

The amount of information available to us is close to infinite. The Internet and our wired lives (after all, you are checking this devotional on an app) make it easy to consume information, even if we don't believe it all. Because of this it's difficult to imagine a time when news traveled by word of mouth, perhaps more likely than in written form. I always think of the game of "telephone" where someone starts a message by whispering it into the ear of someone next to him, and that person passes on what he thinks he heard. But for Rahab, the message was loud, clear, and accurate. She knew what God had done in the lives of the Israelites, and she wanted that for herself and for her family. Think about what you know about God and how that might change what you want for yourself and your friends and family.

Affirmation: You don't have to know the whole Bible to know the story of God.
Prayer: God, help us live out what we already know about You.

Day 8 - God Did What?

My guilty pleasure is reading celebrity news magazines and headlines. Unfortunately, the stories sound crazy, but not so crazy that you wouldn't believe them. Every now and then there is that story that is too crazy to believe and then it turns out to be completely accurate. Sometimes, when I read the Bible it can feel a little like those headlines. How does the water of the Red Sea dry up? How do entire kingdoms fall to lesser armies? Why would God use a prostitute to save the lives of some spies? What God is trying to show in all of these examples is that God will do whatever it takes to show us that we are loved. Through Rahab's story, we see an example of how God never gives up on us and he will always create opportunities to change our lives for the better.

Affirmation: I am not the first person to question God.
Prayer: Thank You, God, for giving space for doubt to help us see the truth.

Day 9 - Family Is Complicated

When given the chance to bargain with the spies, Rahab does a very interesting thing. Instead of securing safety for herself, she makes the spies promise that the lives of her father and mother, her brothers and sisters, and all who belong to them be spared from death. She is a prostitute, and I don't know what kind of relationship she had with her family, but I know that my relationship with my family is complicated enough. Sometimes it's easier for me to think of my own personal well-being and sanity, never mind my parents' or my sister's. But Rahab thinks of the past, current, and the future generations as securing a legacy that is connected to faithfulness and belief in the one true God, but she does not pretend her current situation doesn't exist.

Affirmation: God's love has the power to save even the most complicated family situations.

Prayer: God, help me love my family even when it's difficult and painful.

Day 10 - Numbers Matter

The Bible is a long book with many stories and lots of information. It's easy to pick and choose the stories that we connect with most easily. It's also easy to separate or disconnect stories of the Old Testament from the New Testament. In the Bible, numbers matter. Entire chapters and sometimes even entire books are devoted to keeping record. In Rahab's story, the numeric detail that jumps out is when she tells the spies to hide out in the hills for three days, away from the hustle and bustle of the main road where the king's men would look for them. Three days. Think about the importance of the number three. The Trinity. The number of times Jesus predicts his death. The number of days Jesus' body was in the tomb before He is raised from the dead. How did Rahab know? She didn't.

Affirmation: We don't know how God is writing His story into our lives, but He is.
Prayer: God, help me trust in You, a God of details and consistency.

Day 11 - Your Address Doesn't Determine Your Future

Where we live can have a significant impact on our lives. The quality of your education, access to affordable grocery stores, personal safety, and so on, can all be measured and related to where you reside . We also mistakenly believe those challenges are insurmountable. Rahab literally lived on the edge "for the house she lived in was part of the city wall" (Joshua 2:15). The phrase "living on the edge" can be used to describe someone who takes huge risks as well as someone who is handling all she can handle. Either description fits Rahab's circumstances, right? She is a prostitute living in a culture and time when a woman's future was dependent on marriage. Even as a prostitute, Rahab's survival depended on men. But that didn't matter to God. The spies went straight for what could be a modern neighborhood bar, on the edge of town where everyone knows everyone's business. And there was Rahab not worrying about her address, already thinking about this God of the Israelites she had heard about.

Affirmation: God works everywhere!
Prayer: Dear God, help me to keep my eyes, ears, and heart open to You working everywhere.

Day 12 - Renaming Rahab

It seems everyone knew Rahab. Perhaps it was by reputation, but I wish Rahab had been described as "brave and courageous" because that is what she was. Never mind her occupation. The king sent her a message that basically said, "Look! I know those Israelites went to your place, and you and I both know they are up to no good. Hand them over." That message alone would be a strong incentive to give up the spies. The spies, the king of Jericho, and the king's men all followed orders. They were obedient and maybe loyal, but they weren't extraordinarily brave, though they might have seen themselves that way. That is what is helpful about having another set of eyes on your spiritual journey. You may see yourself one way, but a good friend in the Lord may have another name for you. For Rahab, it would be brave.

Affirmation: I do not have to be known by my mistakes and regrets.
Prayer: God, rename me!

Day 13 - What Are You Listening For?

The world is a noisy place. It doesn't matter whether or not you live in an urban, rural, or suburban community. Cellphones. Advertisements. Street noise. People. Sometimes the noise can be a distraction to hearing, seeing, and recognizing God moving and doing incredible things because we are listening to the wrong things. Rahab, despite living on the fringes of the city and being a woman of questionable reputation, had her ears to the ground and heard stories about God. She could've ignored the stories. Choosing to listen and respond was the difference between life and death.

Affirmation: The stories we hear and see about God moving in our communities can do more than help us survive. They can bring us life.
Prayer: Keep me open to your stories, God.

Day 14 - You and Your + 1

Sometimes it's clear that you and a guest of your choice are being invited to a party. The invitation might read "You and your guest" or "You and _____" but it is completely up to you. The host has given you permission to invite another person. But sometimes you might find yourself in an awkward situation, where you have to stick your neck out to ask for an extra invitation. When Rahab is presented with a chance to save herself, she goes several steps further and asks for her entire family to be saved.

Affirmation: Living a faithful life is a chance to bless others with God's love.
Prayer: Lord God, help me not be selfish but rather share Your blessings!

Day 15 - Don't Be Ashamed

We meet Rahab in the Old Testament as the prostitute who helped the spies in Jericho, but she is not forgotten. We meet her again in the first chapter of Matthew. She is one of only five women mentioned in Jesus' family tree, and one of only four mentioned by name – Tamar, Rahab, Ruth, and Mary. Interestingly enough, all five women in Jesus' family tree (Bathsheba is not mentioned by name but rather as Uriah's wife) were cultural castaways in one way or another, their purity and worth questioned. And yet, they are all mentioned in the genealogy of Jesus Christ even after their stories are told fully! Isn't it something to know that both God's love and His story include real imperfect people with real lives?

Affirmation: God doesn't cast away people, even those who we might cast away ourselves.
Prayer: God, teach me not to be ashamed of what I've done because You are a God of love, forgiveness, and power. You know all things and I worship You.

Day 16- You Don't Know Everything

At first glance I don't think I would've pegged Rahab as knowing a thing about God. She was a prostitute living on the fringes of society. The only people, I would guess, who wanted to be around her had some questionable life experiences as well. I don't usually see people like that at church, but then again I don't know everything about everyone. At first glance, who would've thought Rahab would not only know who the God of Israel was, but that she actually believed and trusted this God; she believed that His spies would protect her from the coming destruction of the city. Romal writes, "Just because people are on the street doing things that could cause them harm or keep them living out from their true purposes doesn't mean they don't believe in God. They really believe in God; the problem is that they don't trust God's people."

Affirmation: It didn't matter that Rahab was a prostitute. What mattered was she believed in God and trusted in God's people.
Prayer: Help me believe in You, God, and trust your people again.

Day 17 - How Can God Use Me?

I grew up in the church. I knew better than to have sex before marriage, but knowing didn't stop me. I knew I would be sinning. No one told me that sin might feel good while also making me feel bad. For years I couldn't get over feeling like I was damaged. I would hear the other boys and girls in youth group talk about the "easy" girls who weren't "pure". (Never mind that I didn't hear anything like that about the boys who also were having sex with the impure girls.) I wasn't a prostitute, but I was just as sinful and ashamed. How could a good Christian boy, let alone someday a young man, see past my past? How could I see past my past? When I look at Rahab I see two things. I see a God who wasn't ashamed of including a prostitute into His story, and I could finally see a young woman who wasn't going to let her past get in the way of a future with God.

Affirmation: I won't let my own shame keep me from God!
Prayer: God, forgive me for my past sins and help me live faithfully now.

Day 18 - What Do You Want?

What gave Rahab the courage and the audacity to ask for a miracle? Who did she think she was asking for not only her safety but for the safety of her entire family? Well, what makes you do crazy things? When you want something desperately for yourself, something you haven't experienced but believe others have, you might do something irrational. I think that's what Rahab did. I think she heard these crazy stories, miracles God was performing for the people of Israel and she wanted in. She wanted to experience that kind of miracle in her life and she was willing to look even more foolish than she already did, if that was possible. She saw the God of miracles and asked for one.

Affirmation: God's love and protection isn't for just the elect few.
Prayer: God, I want to be honest with You. I need a miracle today.

Day 19 - Why Should I Trust You?

Two men come knocking on Rahab's door. Rahab is a prostitute, and it wouldn't surprise me if she thought they were customers. They weren't customers; instead they were two men sent out by God to spy and investigate the land for Joshua. In order for this story to work out well, Rahab has to trust these two men and the men in return have to trust her. Why should a woman trust two strange men who clearly don't belong? Why should two men trust this woman to keep her word? There is so much potential for failure here, and yet that's the situation God sets up. He gives us some crazy choices to make that impact not only our relationship with God, but also have the potential to heal our relationship with others. If we see each other only through the biased opinions we hold of people based on who we think they are, without giving them a chance, we can easily miss an opportunity for our trust in God to heal and save.

Affirmation: Trusting in God first can help us build trust with others.
Prayer: God, help me trust in you even when it's difficult.

Day 20 - What Does a Leader Look Like?

I don't know about you, but when I look at the Bible I see a lot of normal, messed up people who don't fit into the mold of what I thought a leader was, which remained as someone who was almost perfect, has his life together, makes good choices, etc. Some of those leaders acted on their shortcomings. Moses ran when he got caught murdering an Egyptian. King David tried to cover up his rape of another man's wife by trying to have that man murdered. Rahab was a prostitute. I don't know this for sure, but I suspect each of these people had his moment of doubt. In the end, they chose God because they didn't want to keep looking at and living through their past.

Affirmation: My past mistakes do not define my future.
Prayer: God, give me the courage and faith to live into the present and future.

Day 21 - If Rahab Needed Help, So Do You

Romal writes, "The hardest part of learning to trust God is being honest enough with yourself to admit that you need God and courageous enough to not let anything or anyone keep you from seeking God...

33

Trusting God means admitting that you need God." That's exactly what Rahab did. She didn't let her imperfect circumstances make her bitter or completely blind her from recognizing there was no way out. The Israelites were coming to take over her city, and she needed God. She could have been her worst enemy, but instead she chose to have faith in God.

Affirmation: Knowing I need God doesn't mean I am weak. It means I am learning about faith.
Prayer: God, assist me in being honest about my own limitations and help me to seek You first.

Day 22 - I Wouldn't Trust a Prostitute

Honestly, I don't know if I would have trusted Rahab if I had been in that situation. I have a lot of preconceived notions about who is trustworthy, and a prostitute doesn't fall into that category. And if I'm truly honest, I tend to label other people – smart, dumb, ugly, annoying, and worthless -- and that hurts them as much as it hurts me. When we label other people, we refuse to see them as God sees them.

Affirmation: As a Christian, I need to see and value people for the whole of their humanity, just like God sees me.
Prayer: God, help me not be the person labeling and limiting others.

Day 23 - Becoming Neighbors with Your Enemies

Rahab's story doesn't end with her deal with the two spies. After the Israelite army took over the city of Jericho, Joshua sent the two men back to honor the promise made to Rahab; in exchange for her protection, as they spied out the land, they would protect her and all those who belonged to her. The funny thing about obeying God is that you never know when your enemies will stop being enemies and become neighbors. That's exactly what happened to Rahab and the Israelites, because after her city was destroyed, she was given a place among her enemies -- people she had come to trust because of God -- to live out the rest of her days.

Affirmation: God can turn me and my enemies into trusted neighbors.
Prayer: God, bring peace into my broken relationships.

Day 24 - Keep Your Promises

In the heat of war and the destruction of a city, it would have been very easy for Joshua and his men to forget about the promise they made to Rahab, but they didn't. Even as the city of Jericho was being burned to the ground, Joshua made good not just on his word, but also on God's reputation. Rahab trusted the spies because she had heard and believed that the God of Israel was not just her only hope, but that He was also faithful. He who was going to destroy the city would also be the one to deliver her from that destruction. When we make promises as Christians, honoring these commitments say as much about us as it does about God and His faithfulness.

Affirmation: Being faithful and honest isn't always easy or convenient, but if it can be done in a time of war, it can also be done during other times in life.
Prayer: God, I want my words and actions to reflect Your true nature of love and faithfulness.

Day 25 - Why Can't She Just Be Rahab?

I want to know why we have to be reminded that Rahab is a prostitute. Whenever she is mentioned in the book of Joshua, it is in connection with her shady occupation, and that makes me angry. Maybe it's because none of her partners in sin carry that label with them in the Bible, and that can feel like a reminder of her transgression. I don't like being reminded of her sin, let alone of my own. And maybe that's the real problem. I don't want to be reminded that I can't hide my past. I want to be in control of Rahab's reputation and of my own, but that's not the life God is inviting us to. God invited Rahab to give up control and trust, with no guarantees that other people would forget what she did. Maybe erasing the label isn't as important as living faithfully.

Affirmation: Even when I am faithful, I can't change everyone's opinion about my past.
Prayer: God, help me to trust you with my reputation and to live faithfully despite my past.

Day 26 - I Am Not the Only One

When the world is crumbling around you, it's easy to get tunnel vision. It's easy to ask God for a lifeline just so you can get out of a messy situation.

I love that in this messed up situation, Rahab not only thinks about her family, but she also shows kindness. When I get stressed I am usually unkind, short-tempered, selfish, and a bit shortsighted. We see a picture of leadership in Rahab that goes against the world's advice, which essentially says that every woman is for herself. Rahab is wise but decisive. She is kind and clear. She looks for ways to protect her family while offering protection for her "enemies," the spies. She offers a win-win situation. I don't think God picked Rahab on accident. I think He knew she understood leadership in a way we all could learn from.

Affirmation: Leaders don't blaze a trail for themselves. They see opportunities for communities to move forward together.
Prayer: God, create me to be a person who cares for her community.

Day 27 - Plans Change

Rahab didn't set out to aid and abet spies trying to bring ruin to her city. She didn't plan on saving her family. The spies certainly didn't expect a prostitute to be their savior and guide. But everyone had to remain open to the ways God moves, and that requires flexibility and an open heart and mind. They didn't see each other as obstacles. They saw how they would interact with each other as an opportunity to live out faithfulness even though that sometimes requires a change of plans. And look how that worked out for the Israelites and Rahab's family!

Affirmation: Being flexible can open up opportunities I couldn't imagine!
Prayer: God, help me to see obstacles and unexpected changes in my plans as opportunities!

Day 28 - Live What You Know

I don't know how Rahab and the residents of Jericho found out about the faithful and powerful God of Israel, but Rahab didn't just keep the knowledge in her head. She took what she learned about God and applied it to her life. Even though she wasn't Jewish, she took the time to consider how she might join in on what God was doing. Instead of melting in fear like the rest of her city was doing, Rahab saw a God who loved His people and protected them. Might there be such protection for her? She was willing to give it a try and live into the knowledge she had -- she jumped at the opportunity when the spies came to her door.

Affirmation: Applying what I know about God into my life will make faith come alive!
Prayer: God, help me take what I know about You and live it out in my life.

Day 29 - Even When It Couldn't Be Worse There Is Hope

The entire city was cowering in fear because the Israelites were coming to destroy the city, and the only one to have any hope it seems was Rahab, the prostitute. The person who has every reason to give up hope is the one with the most hope. Presumably, Rahab's family also knew about God just like she and the rest of the city, and it was their relationship and proximity to her that saved them. You can't accept Jesus by osmosis, but sometimes when hope is hard to come by, be near people of faith. They can see hope when we have lost our way.

Affirmation: Rahab was a woman of faith who exemplified hope even when circumstances defied hope.
Prayer: God, grant me faith, hope, people around me who can help me when I feel like I've run out.

Day 30 - Some Lessons Are Worth Repeating

I don't know why we have to be reminded repeatedly that Rahab was a prostitute. I would like to think one mention is enough. Why can't we get over the fact that she was a prostitute? Maybe it's not a matter of labeling her. Maybe it's a way to remind us, the readers, that we don't like labels. Maybe we need to be reminded to avoid labeling others and to avoid limiting ourselves because of labels put on us. Maybe it's not about her, but about us because we need to keep learning the lesson.

Affirmation: God is patient and will keep reminding me how He sees me.
Prayer: God, give me the patience and faithfulness to learn about You and live the truth out in my life!

CHAPTER THREE

- JEPHTHAH -

KEVIN ALTON

Day 1 - Off to a Rough Start?

My relationship with God got off to a rough start.

I remember sometime around Christmas of my fifth grade year making a commitment to God. It was a pretty standard realization of my need for a God who was greater than me. I wasn't a bad kid. We weren't well off, but my surroundings were okay. I had a family who loved me and I loved them. I even grew up in church. I just came to a moment where I knew that there was more to life than my own existence, and that my ability to follow the example of Jesus would ultimately be incomplete without God's grace. I probably couldn't have said it like that then, but looking back I know that's what I meant.

But for some reason, that's when the wheels came off my personal life-bus. I'd been a pretty reliable example of a "good kid" at school and church, but that all went away. I started ignoring my schoolwork, either cheating or lying my way through things. I'm pretty certain that I was *placed* in the sixth grade; I can't imagine that my second semester of fifth grade did anything to *earn* it. On top of all that, I started stealing. A lot. From friends, family, and a couple of prominent Floridian vacation tourist traps. Right at the end of the school year I got caught stealing candy at a local grocery store, and my intuitive mother suddenly had the light bulb go on about everything I'd been bringing home all semester labeled, "somebody gave me."

Sometimes stuff just goes sideways in life.

Jephthah's story is a little different than mine; where I could easily (and accurately) have been written off as a petty thief or a school slacker, Jephthah grew up in the shadow of a parent's mistakes (Judges 11:1-3). You might have to be your own advocate, but sometimes simply acknowledging that you're in a tough spot is the first step toward being somewhere else. Jephthah could have wallowed in his circumstances, but he chose to change them.

Affirmation: God knows where I am right now in life and loves me more than I can imagine.

Prayer: God, help me to recognize when it's time to move on from where I am, regardless of how I got there.

Day 2 - Avoiding Negative Labels

We give people labels to save time. Jock. Taxi driver. Soccer mom. Addict. Celebrity. All of these labels allow us to sum up the other person in a word. We don't have to get to know them at all; they're a _____. That's all we need to know.

The dangerous part of labeling people is that it dehumanizes them. And even if we intend some of our labels in a complimentary way—public servant, all-American, even Christian—we've set ourselves up to accept and use negative labels as well.

While *using* negative labels is an external error, *accepting* negative labels is an internal error, one that can follow and dog you for years, if you let it. We tend to accept negative labels on ourselves in places where we already are insecure. Physical appearance, mental capabilities, social standing, or anything that strikes at the core of who we believe we are suddenly feels like a weakness instead of an attribute. We let others define us and then live into those definitions instead of our capability.

What if Jephthah had given in to the labels placed on him and his family? Being born the son of a prostitute hardly made him *unique*. What makes Jephthah unique is how he *overcame* the labels placed on him by his community and culture.

What if we can learn to filter the voices that we allow to define us? What if instead of living defensively we learn to lean into the voice that calls us "beloved"?

Affirmation: I am God's beloved! Whatever anyone else might want to label me, God's love is indelibly written on my soul.
Prayer: God, help me to cling to You—my strength, my place of safety.

Day 3 - Circumstantial Evidence

Even if we're able to put aside what others think or say about us, it can still be difficult to shake the truth of our circumstances when we're trying to figure out who we are in life. If you're growing up in an affluent family with every need attended to and you're never in want of anything, it's hard to see past that reality and understand that people living with less (or none) are equally valuable in God's eyes—and should be equally valuable in your own. If you're growing up with virtually nothing, it can be difficult to believe that your life has value of its own, or that you might one day be able to move beyond those circumstances. Or, you could be right in the middle—just enough to keep you comfortable, not so much that you feel compelled to give any of it away for the sake of another.

Jephthah's circumstances were difficult, to be sure. It's the most natural response imaginable to believe that the circumstances into which you're born are meant to define who you are—why wouldn't they? We're raised to understand that our life's outcomes are a result of the decisions we make, but for some reason we aren't often encouraged to examine the circumstances we encounter that are the result of someone else's decisions. We don't need to throw away everything we were born into, but we need to feel free to seek what God might have for us beyond those circumstances.

Affirmation: I am meant to be all that God created me to be! I am defined by *who* I am and *whose* I am, not by anything in my surroundings.
Prayer: God, help me to daily seek what you have specially equipped me to be. Help me use my life to honor You.

Day 4 - Love Your Neighbor

Romal reflects on an unfortunate truth in Chapter 3: "People can be harsh, mean, unfair, and unforgiving." In the devotion for Day 2, we talked about how important it is to not allow yourself to accept negative labels from others, but there's an important corresponding truth in the way that we're called to live our lives as followers of Jesus. *We* cannot be harsh, mean, unfair or unforgiving. We can't use negative labels. We have to be the better person, even if it's at our own expense.

Why? Because we're trying to be like Jesus. That doesn't mean we won't fail from time to time. In fact, we certainly *will* fail from time to time, and time again. But we can't live in the duplicity of claiming to be a Christ-follower around our Christian friends and then do whatever we want with our other friends. Or, even worse, do whatever we want around people that we don't know at all.

I learned a long time ago to start paying attention to the people in the margins of my life. Gas station attendants. Waiters and waitresses.

Service persons of all shapes and sizes. Even just strangers who I seem to bump into from time to time. You'll be amazed at the opportunities that will present themselves when you try to live out your faith around *everyone*. I don't mean that you have to unload your spiritual journey on them. Just learn to love your neighbor.

Affirmation: I have the opportunity to be Jesus to people who otherwise might never know that love.
Prayer: God, let me overcome my selfish desires and be willing to spread your love in every area of my life.

Day 5 - Not All Abuse Makes the News

There's really no telling what Jephthah saw or experienced as he grew up. The way his mom made her living certainly exposed him to some rough circumstances. It's doubtful that he grew up with a healthy, meaningful relationship with her. At a minimum, his moral compass would have been a little off kilter. It's amazing what we're capable of overcoming.

You may have suffered abuse that's simply not as "popular," though that may be an odd word to throw at it. Not all abuse is obvious to the people around you. Not all abuse involves addiction. Not all abuse is physical. Some abuse is mental and some abuse is self-inflicted. The key to recognizing it is to frame everything that you do, feel, and experience against the powerful love of God.

If you find yourself aware that there are things you're doing to yourself, or things that others are doing to you, that seem contrary to what you've felt in God's love, call it out. Talk to someone. Change your environment, if you can. Be honest with yourself and God about what you're feeling—God can take it.

Affirmation: I don't have to live with abuse! I claim the love of God in my life.
Prayer: God, show me where I can help others identify and live for change in situations involving abuse of all kinds.

Day 6 - Staying Warm When Life Goes Cold

As a youth worker, I'm continually reminding my kids that the meanest, toughest (or sometimes biggest) jerks that they know in school are very likely also the most tender and most wounded people they'll ever meet. In general,

I insist on kindness from our group; you never know when your light-hearted jab will be the knife that their day just didn't need. Mom yelled at Steve before he left the house this morning; you made fun of his shirt. The risk may seem small, but why not err on the side of being loving? It's way more likely that someone will need a kind or supportive comment in his or her day.

Jephthah's environment growing up shaped him into a hard person. He had a tough personality that was necessary to survive the difficult home environment in which he was raised (Judges 11:3). Showing emotions, like sadness, would have been a sign of weakness; any show of emotion would have unlocked all that he felt about his mom and the way he was treated.

A word of caution: bottling emotion will wreck you. Not only does it change who you are, it changes *how* you are. If you're bitter about not receiving love, you'll find it nearly impossible to love others. If you've grown up in an unacknowledged unforgiving environment, you'll find it difficult to even understand forgiveness. Both of those situations will complicate your relationships not only with other people, but with God as well.

Affirmation: Who I am in God's eyes is more important than my surroundings or how others treat me.
Prayer: God, bathe me in your love and forgiveness, even when I don't feel either from those around me.

Day 7 - A Chip off the Old Block

"The apple doesn't fall far from the tree" and about 1,000 other expressions indicate that who we are and how we approach others in relationships are a swirl of genetics and learned behavior from our parents. I've been a parent for nearly 10 years now and (often with deep chagrin) I hear myself saying things that my father or mother would say to us as kids, and those things go way beyond the "I'll turn this car right around" or "Because I said so" sayings. I'm speaking here of core-level stuff like "Let's just keep on trucking" (from Mom) when one of my sons feigns illness trying to avoid school, or "I didn't ask a question" (from Dad) when reemphasizing a parental command.

Jephthah's primary input from his family was hurt. All of the abuse and shame and distance from real love from his mom shaped him into a hurting person. And the main skill set engrained into hurt people is the ability to hurt others.

What about you? Are you a hurt person? Or, are you a loved person? Have you ever bothered to consider how your environment growing up shaped you as a person? It's a natural progression for you to let how you were shaped affect how you shape others that you're in relationship with. Not just kids, but loved ones, friends, even (and perhaps especially) strangers.

Affirmation: I am free to be the person God has created me to be. I can choose which parts of my past I want to pass on to others.
Prayer: God, I know that you love me. Let me only extend to others the ways that I am shaped by you.

Day 8 - Beating Your Bullies

Well, not actually beating them, though that might be your inclination.

The only class I even came close to failing in middle school was seventh grade history. I got a D, probably due to some kind of mercy rule. I don't remember what kind of history the class covered; in my defense, I *did* just tell you I got a D. I had the staggering misfortune of sitting in the front left corner of the classroom, trapped between the two championship-level seventh grade bullies, David Jackson and Eddie Doty. David dressed like Michael Jackson when that was still cool and he could bench-press well over 100 pounds. Eddie wore a lot of Iron Maiden T-shirts and was old enough that he started driving to school in the eighth grade. I was doomed. Between pokes, punches, books getting kicked out of under my desk, and an endless stream of questions intended to get a rise out of me, I just didn't learn a lot about history that year.

The school climate has changed somewhat, and bullies seem to be more readily identified and dealt with by school administration. But the problem still persists in back hallways and bus rides. Even worse, as we get older we realize that the bullies don't ever really go away: attitudes and actions of co-workers and people we encounter in public take us right back to that childhood tension of being pushed around.

There is hope! Jephthah had to overcome his childhood experiences, too. We're capable of doing the same. Not only can we survive, but we can succeed in spite of the things that could have held us down.

Affirmation: I am not called to live a life of fear. I am called to excel in my circumstances.
Prayer: God, show me the way beyond the bullies I encounter in life, both real and imagined.

Day 9 - Strength from Weakness

Marriage is a funny thing. When I was a kid, I believed that how happy a couple was together determined how long they'd remain together. As an adult, I've come to realize that a marriage that lasts tells you one thing— that couple has found their way through some hard times. There are no life lessons in being gaga in love or living through good times. *Anybody* can do that. Where marriage really cuts its teeth is how it navigates the things that *end* marriages. If you know a couple who have been married for any length of time, you can be assured they've lived through some real stuff.

Character develops the same way. If Jephthah had grown up in a storybook family situation, we might never have heard of him. It doesn't require any resolve to live through good times nor do you learn anything particularly useful when times are good. It's when life comes at you hard that you develop grit and determination.

Rather than feeling like you need to hide your struggles, consider what you've been through in life as an opportunity to help others find their way through their own difficult times. You'll be amazed at how much relief others will find in the camaraderie of someone who has faced similar difficulties.

Affirmation: Who I am is the sum of what I have experienced! God can use my story to help others find words for their own.
Prayer: God, may I let go of any shame or negativity about my past, realizing that you can use even that to bring others closer to you.

Day 10 - Forgiving the Past

Forgiveness is hard.

Sometimes you just don't want to forgive someone; it's a totally natural response. Sometimes you're afraid to talk to them. What if they don't acknowledge that they've wronged you in any way? What if they reject your forgiveness? Is your forgiveness about releasing them from wrongdoing or about releasing yourself from hanging on to hatred or resentment? What does forgiveness do, anyway?

For Romal, forgiveness released him from shame that wasn't his. Like Jephthah, his mother's choices in life had placed him in dire circumstances. To free him to be who God intended him to be, he had to let go of where life had placed him, releasing himself and his mother from any responsibility to that negative place. Forgiveness didn't remove the reality of the situation, but it removed the power that situation held over Romal.

Where do *you* need to forgive? Are there places that you need to forgive yourself? What's stopping you? For a Christian, the practice and understanding of forgiveness plays a huge part in our relationship with God. Through forgiveness, we understand our need for, and ability to receive, grace. Through forgiveness, we can begin to repair relationships with those whom we are called to live in community. Through forgiveness we can become more like Christ, whose disciples we claim to be.

Affirmation: I forgive myself for the places where I need forgiveness, and I will work to forgive others for the things I know I haven't forgiven.
Prayer: God, thank You so much for Your forgiveness. And, thank You for Your grace. Help me to extend both to those that I know I should extend them to.

Day 11 - Embrace Your Gifts

If we've become accustomed to forever trying to disentangle ourselves from our past or pulling ourselves up out of circumstances we don't deserve, it's easy to forget that God has more for us in life than simply escaping a train-wreck existence. We can achieve things! We can excel! We can lead!

Yet to accomplish things and take action, we must recognize the gifts that God has placed within each of us. Instead of overcoming weaknesses today, focus on what your strengths are. What are you naturally good at? What do you do well? What are you passionate about? What passions can you inspire in others?

Jephthah moved from being a downtrodden Israelite to a key protector of the nation (Judges 11:11). It didn't happen overnight, but over time he was able to realize that he had strengths as a leader. It didn't mean that he'd made his last mistakes, but he'd made great strides in moving away from the pain of his past to a place where he could return good things to the very people that had once treated him poorly. What a transformation!

Affirmation: I am uniquely gifted! There are things about me that can allow me to help and lead others that no one else possesses in the way that I do.
Prayer: God, I want to overcome my past and use all that You have given to me to make a difference in the world around me.

Day 12 - Freedom in the Future

It's really amazing what we can accomplish once we start living for the future instead of clinging to our past.

I've got a good friend who's a golf professional. Not a professional golfer; those guys are the millionaires that you see on TV on the weekends. My friend is a "thousand-aire" who works at a private golf course as a PGA club pro. He plays in competitive events a few times a year, and on a few occasions I've caddied for him, carrying his bag and walking with him through the highs and lows of competitive play.

The first time I caddied for him was at the Tennessee State Open, which includes both pros like him and excellent amateurs. The prize for winning was $10,000, which is nothing to sneeze at. Being a caddy is a nervous place to be; you've got to know your golfer's temperament and when it's okay to joke and when it's better to shut up. My friend had a good round going, but on a hole late in the round, he'd hit a poor shot that cost him a couple of strokes. On the next tee, a par 3, he stood glaring back at the previous hole. I could tell he was replaying the bad shot over and over in his mind. I let him do it for a minute, but then touched his shoulder and said, "I don't think there's anything you can do about that shot. And I'm pretty sure we're playing in this direction," pointing at the hole ahead, 180 degrees from where he was staring.

He later said that moment completely changed the way he approached a round of golf. He stated he almost always stood staring back at mistakes instead of looking ahead to see what he could make of what was next. As Jephthah learned, success in life is about more than escaping the past— it's about living for the future.

Affirmation: My future is worth more to my life as a Christ-follower than anything that may have happened in my past.
Prayer: God, help me learn what I can from my past and leave the rest to You. Help me to celebrate the opportunity to honor You with my future!

Day 13 - You Have Got to Move

Moving is a hard thing at any age. Typically it means leaving behind old friends and relationships. While adults are capable of reasoning that the new location will bring new friends and community, even they often face the transition with some trepidation. Change is hard.

What makes change even more difficult is when it's necessary. More to the point, it's more difficult when you're changing not because you *want* to but because you *have* to. Change is necessary when you're in an unhealthy environment. Change is necessary when you're trying to create distance between the way you once lived and the way you're feeling called to live. Sometimes you need new geography and sometimes you need new community around you. Both are tough.

Jephthah needed new friends. He quickly found new community, albeit with a band of outlaws (Judges 11:3). But that movement beyond his childhood circumstances would eventually allow him to return as a welcome hero.

Affirmation: I value myself as a person of God enough that I am willing to change my present circumstances if it will improve my relationship with God. **Prayer:** God, thank You for the places in life that give me strength. Help me to recognize the places that weaken me.

Day 14 - Fearless Through Fear

Before I began a fulltime youth ministry career, I was an avid kayaker. I'd arrive at church most Sunday mornings with my boat in the back of my pickup, ready to head out to the Ocoee River before the pastor could finish saying, "In the name of the Father, in the name of the..." I was pretty relentless about it.

Before I was an avid kayaker, I was a deeply terrified kayaker. Something about the potential of being trapped upside down under water with my lower half sealed in a boat just didn't sit well with me. I enjoyed the camping part of our trips and even the flat water, but the rapids made me freeze up inside. The idea of intentionally playing in a wave or hydraulic was so overwhelming that I put stick-on letters on the back of my helmet spelling "Chicken" so that anyone in line behind me at a play spot would at least understand the delay. I was so excited when I finally felt competent enough to upgrade both my helmet and the difficulty of river I could paddle.

Jephthah wasn't born fearless, nor were his friends. Presuming their backgrounds were anything like his, they had to overcome a lot of fear to become fearless. My fearlessness finally met its match—an underwater concussion ultimately ended my resolve to be on the river. How have you met your fears successfully? Where have you let them get the better of you?

Affirmation: I can learn from *everything* in my life. God can work all things in my life for good.

Prayer: God, show me how I can use even things that intimidate or frighten me to become points of strength in my life.

Day 15 - A Need to Belong

When I was a little kid—maybe in third or fourth grade—I started a bike club for the kids in my neighborhood. I planned monthly meetings, established an application process, recorded an audio presentation for new member initiation meetings, and created a t-shirt to be worn on club rides, adventures, and service projects. It was awesome.

The only problem was that the club only existed in my brain. I did create the audio presentation (on cassette, baby) and ruined an undershirt with a permanent marker bringing a T-shirt to life. There was even a poorly crafted wooden box I mashed together with a slit in the lid for... donations? Suggestions? Who knows? I was ready for all manner of things that would never come to be. But the idea of the thing was born out of a need to belong.

Romal notes that many street gangs form out of similar desires for community. Jephthah's crew wasn't looking to join anything violent or rebellious; they were simply reaching out for something familiar—a place to be accepted and valued -- offering a sense of protection and belonging.

Where have you found your own sense of belonging? Did finding that place represent a major life change, or were you able to find it in your natural environment growing up?

Affirmation: All the sense of belonging I need can be found in communion with God.

Prayer: God, let my life lead others into deeper communion with You. May I be an active participant in Your community here on earth?

Day 16 - Hiding Who You Are

The description of Romal's violent induction into gang life might be disturbing to some. The idea of being *beaten* into community sounds antithetical to the concept of community, but it's not uncommon in the process of gang initiation. Getting *out* of gang life is often even more physically unappealing. But the willingness to endure it suggests the depth of desire for acceptance.

The odd aftermath of Romal's induction is that he hid his new identity and community from his family. They eventually figure it out as he had changed how he dressed and wore gang colors. But, on the details of his induction he remained silent.

What do you hide about who you *really* are? Are there things that you'd say in person or on social media that you refrain from based on the opinion of family? Friends? Work relationships or expectations? Do you hide those things because deep down you're not certain that they're good things, or because you just don't want to make waves in your daily life?

Hiding who you really are can be a steady drain on your mental and physical energy! There are situations in life where being "you" unfiltered isn't appropriate, but if it's a daily habit, spend some time thinking about what's holding you back. Are you limiting what God is calling you to be, or are you living in a way that perhaps you need to reconsider?

Affirmation: I am God's creation; I should feel free to be me.
Prayer: God, please help me discover my motivations for hiding parts of "me" when I feel compelled to do so. Help me find the strength to always be willing to reveal the parts of me that are most like You.

Day 17 - Doing Whatever It Takes

What does "whatever it takes" look like for you? Giving it all you've got? Are you willing to break rules? To cheat, if necessary? Doesn't sound very Christian, does it?

But look at Jephthah. Or Romal. Or yourself. Funny how necessity can seem to transcend reality or morality or any ordinary sense of Christian duty at times, doesn't it? Have you ever had a moment where you felt that your Christian duty compelled you to side step the rules of society? What were those circumstances?

Let's face it: rules are weird. They give us order, they protect us at times, and they give us reasonable expectations about the behavior of others. But, there are times that rules aren't applicable for the present circumstances, like when a fire truck screams through a red light. The rules are in the way of something more important.

This isn't an encouragement to discard the rules in your life. The flip side of rule breaking is consequence; any time you feel inclined to side step a rule, you've got to weigh the outcome against the penalty for doing so. For Jephthah, survival must have trumped all rules as he and his friends endured the wilderness.

Affirmation: I have the strength to "do whatever it takes" to follow after God.
Prayer: God, grant me the discernment to know when my actions need to answer to You and You alone.

Day 18 - Making a Deal with God

How many times have you bargained with God? "If you'll get me out of this mess, I'll gladly _____ for the rest of my life!!" We see that transaction mentality over and over again in movies, books, and the lives of our friends, family, and even our own approach to existence. We're fully willing to wheel and deal to enlist any power greater than our own to satisfy the need of a moment.

I can remember when I was a kid setting up ridiculous agreements with my brothers, promising months of desserts for an afternoon with a specific toy, or getting to choose what we'd watch on TV that day. I could work the other side, too, demanding impossible gains from my brothers that cost me very little. We had chores as kids, and doing those for each other was a ready unit of exchange on the free market of our deal making.

Jephthah's time of survival in the wilderness was no doubt filled with that kind of bartering. His instincts from that time appear to have affected his approach to a relationship with God. Rather than asking for favor or protection or even a peaceful resolution, Jephthah bargains foolishly with a God who never wished to bargain (Judges 11:30).

Affirmation: God desires nothing from me but love—both for God and others.
Prayer: God, remind me daily that I'm not "plan B." Help me to think of You as more of a companion than an ally.

Day 19 - Alone in the Crowd

We're born for community. Even the most introverted people have a desire to be around others with whom they can exchange love and trust. A big part of that desire arises from an inner longing to connect with the Spirit of God. But we need healthy relationships around us to support us, guide us, and even correct us when necessary.

When we find the relationships in our immediate surroundings unfulfilling, it's natural to go looking for them elsewhere. Romal looked to the gangs in his neighborhood for acceptance. In a way, that acceptance existed there—but with heavy conditions. Ultimately, he would have to change who he wanted to be as a person to continue to be accepted by them.

The acceptance God offers is unconditional. And despite all of the different ways that people approach and understand God, there's a loving community there too that wants to support you. Don't go looking for community, but rather, find the community that's looking for you.

Affirmation: I am loved without condition by God, and I am accepted exactly as I am.
Prayer: God, help me to find the answers that I seek in living my life to honor You.

Day 20 - More than You Bargained for

Any sales pitch starts with what the advertiser thinks that you want to hear. One low price, bundled services. Then they entice you: for a limited time only, just this weekend, and so on. The appeal is strong and we are weak. As a population trained to consume, we've acclimated ourselves to jumping on what seems appealing on the surface without investigating what it might cost us later.

As an example, I dare you to figure out what switching to a new cable/internet provider will cost you in your thirteenth month of service. They'll tell you all about the low introductory rate, cough to the side about a two-year contract, and dazzle you with movies that magically follow you through the house. But at some point the fairy dust will settle and you'll be faced with the *real* bill, which is probably double or more of what you were paying the month before.

In Romal's case, there wasn't any fine print to read and contracts were worked out physically rather than financially. His new community that had seemed so appealing quickly turned into a nightmare of violence, drugs, and weapons, all flirting with an undesirable relationship with law enforcement.

When have you gotten in over your head? What circumstances led you there? What was the result?

Affirmation: I value myself enough to consider the cost of *anything* that I might choose to involve myself.
Prayer: God, help me to seek You first, always. Guide me in my decisions.

Day 21 - The Road to Nowhere

When I first went to college, I went for the same reason as most of my peers: obligation. You're supposed to go to college, right? I wasn't the first in my family to go; I wasn't even the smartest in my family. I grew up in a world where most jobs with any kind of future had "…and a college degree" tagged onto the end of the list of qualifications. Many less specialized jobs didn't even care what your degree was—they just wanted you to have been to "higher education." As an example, youth ministry resumes are littered with liberal arts and history degrees. Nothing to do with ministry, but hey, they went to college.

Romal points out the importance of being honest with yourself and those around you if you want to become a leader. For years I wasn't; I changed majors like most people change socks. I changed from Music to Music & Christian Education to Bible to dropping out for a year to Business to Journalism to English, with an eye on teaching. Eventually, my wife kindly suggested we give college a rest until I was a little more certain about what I wanted to do in life.

Sixteen years after I graduated from high school, I completed a Bachelor of Science in Ministry Studies. I'd finally returned to the call I'd felt in high school. I was finally honest with myself about how I could best use the gifts I'd been given.

Affirmation: I am worth the time it takes to get to know myself.
Prayer: God, show me what you have created me to be capable of accomplishing.

Day 22 - Feeling Courageous

I'm a singer. But, for years I was uncomfortable saying that. I sang in church choirs when I was little, but when I got older and learned to play guitar, I just stuck with that through all of the bands I was ever in. It wasn't until I began serving in youth ministry full time that singing became necessary; a youth minister who plays guitar is naturally also expected to sing. Even then, I wouldn't call myself a singer, I'd say, "worship leader" or find some other way around it.

The thing that I didn't like about singing was the vulnerability it required. My voice sounds like my voice, and there's not much I can do about it one way or another. If you don't like the way I play guitar, that's fine by me. I decided what style of guitar playing I wanted to pursue; if I wanted, I could even learn a style that you did like. But my voice is part of *who* I am—if you don't like it, there's nothing I can do about it. And if I find out you don't like it, your dislike will feel personal. You don't like something about *me*.

The courage Romal talks about regarding sharing your emotions involve overcoming the same fears I had about singing in front of people. Your emotions are tied to the core of your being; if someone rejects them, it feels like they're rejecting you. That's where the courage part comes in—you've got to have the strength to believe in who you are enough to express yourself to others. You're uniquely made. Embrace that.

Affirmation: I have value as an individual—my feelings matter.
Prayer: God, show me how I can express my emotions and accept the emotions of others at the same time.

Day 23 - It's up to You

Romal is repeatedly asked how he escaped the circumstances that could so easily have reframed his existence, confining him to a life wrapped up in violence and personal destruction. Each of the issues he faced required a different response, a different process. But they all held one thing in common: Romal had to want that thing to change. Some were within his control, some weren't. His first step, though, in each instance was the desire and willingness to do whatever it took to change.

You don't have to wait to hit rock bottom to make change in your life. You don't even have to be in the difficult places that Romal or Jephthah found themselves in. Easier surroundings can actually make you stay in an unhealthy or unsubstantial place longer; if life isn't that difficult, why bother pursuing something better?

Hopefully you don't have to go it alone. Maybe you already have a relationship with God from which you can draw strength. Maybe you've got a good friend or two, or family member, to help you along. But change begins with you.

My family has recently made the decision to leave our local church, where my wife and I were both employed. This was purely in response to God's movement in our lives; our circumstances were pretty great, certainly nothing you'd want to escape from. In its own way, our situation took guts and determination too. I can assure you, feeling called away from what looks like security doesn't make for easy first steps, either.

Affirmation: With God's help, I can boldly step out to whatever is next for me.
Prayer: God, thank You so much for Your presence. May I take Your spirit with me into every decision and motivation?

Day 24 - You Can Run, But You Can't Hide

Fight or flight. This common description of our response to certain stressors is remarkably accurate in such few words. When we feel attacked, cornered, or just like we need to escape, our innate instinct is to either defend our ground or hightail it out of here like our feet are on fire.

Jephthah made the decision to leave (Judges 11:3). Was it the right decision? Who knows? All we know is that it was the decision he made. His story, the one we read in scripture, tells us the result of his decision. If he'd stayed put, would he ever have learned to fight? If he'd never learned to fight, would his daughter not have paid the cost of a careless bargain?

Which path would God have chosen for Jephthah?

The thing is, God wants us to make decisions. We've been given incredible abilities to perceive and assess and act. We are *created* for decision-making. God has equipped us to trust our ability to decide when it's best to stick it out where we are, and when it's better to move on to something or somewhere new. And by making a decision, we've shown our trust in God—because God created us! Get it?

Affirmation: I am so incredibly equipped to live this life. I can trust that God has prepared me for even this day.
Prayer: I love You, God! Thank You so much for all of the potential You've placed within me.

Day 25 - Don't Believe the Lie

Haters, as they say, are going to hate.

But you don't have to believe them. I saw a wonderful quadrant diagram online about the proper placement of haters. One corner was designated for people who love you and would never speak ill of anything you might say or do. Another was set-aside for people who loved you but would be willing to offer genuinely useful and well-intentioned criticism. A third was labeled for those who might dislike you, but would still be still capable of offering reasonable critique or advice. The last, naturally, was dubbed "haters," and was reserved for those who wouldn't like anything about you, your words, or your actions, no matter what. Haters are going to hate.

But if you're like me, the haters are the voices you tend to listen to. They agree with everything that you dislike about yourself; your own negativity affirms their disregard of everything about you.

STOP IT. The haters are shallow cowards, afraid to engage you as a person, reflecting their own negativity into you and others so that they don't have to deal with the things that they don't like about themselves. You are God's person. Believe in that.

Affirmation: God has covered me in grace; no other judge in this life can bear sentence over me.
Prayer: Thanks be to the God who loves and redeems! I praise You for the truth of goodness that You have placed within me.

Day 26 - Real Change Happens on the Inside

Romal and his mom moved all the time, from neighborhood to neighborhood to neighborhood. Every time they moved probably felt like a chance for a fresh start, but he shares that in the end, after each move, he would eventually hang out with the same kind of crowd, in the same kind of places, doing the same kinds of things as he did in his previous places of residency. Changing your address only changes where packages arrive. It doesn't change *you* at all.

I grew up in the suburbs of Atlanta, a northern transplant having been born in Rhode Island and raised by parents from Jersey. When I was in the fifth grade, my parents spent a lot of time talking about moving, buying some land, and building a house. Even though it would have meant changing school systems, my older brother and I were a little excited about the idea of a new start. We weren't exactly at the bottom of the social order, but we felt that our gradual awareness that there *was* a social order somehow might position us—with just a little effort—to land a little higher on the ladder somewhere else. The idea that we'd be helping to build the house also sparked the imagining of newly tanned, muscular selves hitting the sixth and seventh grade scenes.

In reality, we ended up renting a house somewhere new, which was not quite as exciting as we had imagined. Worse for me, in the new school system, elementary school extended through the sixth grade, which meant that instead of the excitement of entering a new level of education, I was stuck in the old one.

None of that made a bit of difference in who I actually was, though it would take years for me to figure that out.

Affirmation: I have the ability to change, but I must realize that real change comes from within, not by altering external circumstances.
Prayer: God, I want to be Your person in this world. If I need to be different than I am, help me to make those changes.

Day 27 - No Seriously, You Can Actually Be Anything

I don't care what age you are. If you could redefine your life right now on your own terms, what would change? How would you dress? What would you do?

For an introvert, I've spent way too much time thinking about my personal appearance. Some of it is my case-study blend of obsessive-compulsive disorder, giftedness, and depression. The combination of these gives you a superpower of noticing absolutely everything about yourself, hyper-analyzing that, and then being rainy day dissatisfied with all of it in varying degrees. And, I know that one of my eyes looks more squinty than the other through my glasses due to the massive difference in my left and right eye prescriptions. (I walked into a pine tree as a kid, poking the mess out of my right eye.) And, I also know that I can spread my fingers on my left hand significantly farther apart than on my right hand as a result of years of playing guitar; my left hand has been trained to stretch farther, reaching for chords not required by my pick-holding right hand. In addition, I'm aware that I'm healthier at forty-one than I've been in my entire life, even if you include the onset of Type 1 diabetes in the last month and a half.

All of that said, the self-re-imaginations of my youth have faded in importance. I care more about respiratory fitness than any form of muscular appearance. I'll ride a bicycle for days and never pick up a weight. I'll quit a youth ministry job with a pension in favor of finding out what God seems to want for me next. I'm more attuned spiritually than I've ever been.

Like Romal says, I've changed my attitude and lifestyle to fit my goals. My goals are no longer self-centered -- they're God-centered.

Affirmation: I'm free to re-imagine my life beyond my present circumstances—the challenge is to keep God at the center of that re-imagining.
Prayer: God, I need You to be at my center, so that all I imagine stems from You.

Day 28 - Finding New Voices

Here we're a little out of my personal experience and into my observation over years of work with youth in ministry. I can't count the times that I've seen a young person make a genuine effort to change who they are for God, or even just for themselves, and get stuck because they couldn't bring themselves to leave behind influential voices that were holding them back.

I've been fortunate, personally. Most of the voices in my life have been positive and assuring, so, what I've had to overcome has been *myself*. You may be more like me than Romal in that regard. If that's the case, whom can you help? The times that I've felt I'm most fulfilling my call to youth ministry have been times where I reached back and helped someone else find their inner strength, their ability to listen to new voices.

This isn't a tough self-assessment; you're either a person in a position of need or you're a person in a position to help someone else. What are you willing to do to act on either of those positions?

Affirmation: I am either in need of, or able to provide, a new guiding voice.
Prayer: God, help me to discern my position. If I am able to help others, guide them to me. If I need the help of others, guide me to them.

Day 29 - The Patience to Change

I feel certain that there are teen movies I have not seen (probably several) that center on the idea that the girl, once despised by her peers, is suddenly called upon to lead them to safety or a better understanding of themselves or the greatest prom theme ever. Obviously, teenage girls are profoundly more capable than any of these themes would suggest, but that is what happens when they're reduced to marketable film.

What's required in those movies (I presume, having not seen them) of the main, once-despised character, is the patience to change, or, at the very least, the patience to wait for and then accept change in her former adversaries.

Jephthah is the despised teenage girl. He's *like* the teenage girl. And like the teenage girl, Jephthah didn't just yell, "Yay!" and jump into a requested leadership role. Jephthah had to dig deep. These people had hurt him; they'd rejected him, and they'd insulted his mother. Why on earth would he even consider helping them?

We've all heard the saying, "God moves in mysterious ways," which sometimes means that God moves in ways that we can't understand. And, sometimes it means that God is moving *us* in ways that we can't understand.

Forgiving the past is one of the hardest things you'll ever do. You'll have to decide what things you need to deal with face to face, and then you'll need to decide what things you need to just let pass, like water under the bridge. And you'll also need God to give you the patience to know the difference.

Affirmation: I'm not able to forgive my past on my own; this is strength, not a weakness. There is a God greater than I am who can walk with me through the decisions and processes that involve my past.
Prayer: Lord, be my strength. Be my weakness. Be my forgiveness. Be all of those things when I cannot.

Day 30 - Letting Go

After any great success achieved by our heroes of scripture, there seems to immediately follow a moment of reckoning, a time of poor decision or unfortunate consequence. David has been successful at war, then stays home and finds Bathsheba. Elijah defeats the prophets of Baal and immediately flees to a cave, lamenting that he alone stands in defense of God. And, Jephthah almost preemptively throws his family under the bus, negotiating success at the expense of whoever might greet him on return from victory.

What about putting faith in God and letting the rest sort itself out? Why are we so inclined to pile up offerings of "and this, and this" in exchange for what *we* want?

I once bargained with God for everything I thought that I wanted in life. This grade. This girl. This guitar. This job. This whatever. In an ultimate irony, I eventually, and gratefully, handed over my very existence—without condition—to a God that I know beyond a shadow of a doubt that I will never fully understand. And I've never been more satisfied in life.

Jephthah didn't quite get to that point of total belief or release; in the end he bargained the life of his daughter beyond any request of God and sacrificed her beyond any wish of God.

Affirmation: I must let go of my past to the point that I can trust God in my present. **Prayer**: God, may I find my strength only in You—never in myself. May You always be enough for me.

CHAPTER FOUR

- ISHMAEL -

SHAWN CASSELBERRY

Day 1 - It's Not Fair

Life is unfair. That is the theme of Ishmael's life. He gets a raw deal. His stepbrother, Isaac, is loved and given a place of special privilege by his father Abraham while he is kicked out on the street. Ishmael and Isaac had the same father, but they grew up in different worlds. Isaac grew up advantaged while Ishmael grew up disadvantaged. Why are some born into wealth and others born into poverty? Why do some have more than they need to live well while others do not have nearly what they need to survive? Twenty percent of the world's population uses 80 percent of the world's resources. Likewise, 80 percent of the world's population survives on 20 percent of the world's resources. The world is not fair. What do we do about this kind of inequality in our world? What is God's response? Even though Abraham rejects Ishmael, God doesn't. God shows concern for those who are treated unfairly. Isaac is promised to become a mighty nation. God promises that Ishmael will become a great nation, too. Even though the world is unfair, God seeks to even the playing field. Whether you grew up in advantage or disadvantage, God has plans for you.

Affirmation: God has plans for my life.
Prayer: Lord, help me care for those who are treated unfairly.

Day 2 - You Are Not a Mistake

God promised Abraham and Sarah a son, but they got impatient. Instead of waiting for God's timing and God's promise, Abraham slept with his servant Hagar. Abraham chose to act out of God's will and Ishmael was conceived. After this, Abraham and Sarah did conceive Isaac. Although Abraham acted out of God's will, God does not cast Ishmael away. In God's eyes, no human life is a mistake. When a new life comes into the world, they are automatically given purpose. No one is cast aside. The circumstances surrounding Ishmael's birth did not cancel out God's purpose for him. Whatever the circumstances surrounding your birth—whether you were planned by your parents or not, whether both your parents were around or not—you have purpose. God told the prophet Jeremiah, "Before I formed you in the womb

61

I knew you, and ordained you a prophet to the nations" (Jeremiah 1:5). God also knew you before you were formed in the womb. You are not a mistake. The God of Abraham, Isaac, and Jacob is also the God of Ishmael.

Affirmation: I have purpose.
Prayer: O God, You are my God, and I will forever praise You.

Day 3 - Family Drama

Ishmael's life is like an episode of the "Maury" show; there's some serious drama here. Sarah urges her husband Abraham to sleep with his servant Hagar so they can have a son. After the son is conceived, they decide to kick the servant and her child out of the house. This is a very messed-up situation. In some ways, it's kind of nice to see some dysfunctional families in the Bible. It can help us feel better about our own families! It also helps me believe these stories are probably true. If you were making up stories about the heroes of the faith, you would probably not include all the messy details. But the Bible keeps it real, reflecting the brokenness of our human world. All you have to do is turn on the news or daytime television to see that the world is filled with family drama. It's universal. But just because we have family drama, it doesn't mean we can't grow up and become healthy adults. Isaac and Ishmael both go on to accomplish their purpose. Overcoming their family drama, they did not let their past hinder where God was leading them. All of our families are dysfunctional in some ways, but the story of Ishmael shows us that God is able to work through even the most dysfunctional families.

Affirmation: I am not the only one with family drama.
Prayer: God, do not let my family background hinder me from pursuing Your purpose for me.

Day 4 - Who Are You?

If your past doesn't define you, who are you?
If your family doesn't define you, who are you?
If where you are born doesn't define you, who are you?
If you are not what you accomplish, who are you?
If you are not what you have, who are you?
If you are not what others think about you, who are you?
If you are not how much money you make, who are you?
If you are not your worst mistakes, who are you?

If you are not an accident of nature, who are you?
Psalm 139 says you are "fearfully and wonderfully made."
You are a child of God.
Ephesians 5:1 notes that we are "dearly loved children."
You are "created for good works." (Ephesians 2:10)
Where will you find your identity?
Who do you think you are?

Affirmation: I am a child of God.
Prayer: Lord, help me find my identity and worth in You.

Day 5 - What Gives Your Life Meaning?

We are meaning makers. One of the things that make the human species unique is that we are able to make meaning out of our world. Animals live by instincts. They eat; they mate; they die. We, on the other hand, are constantly searching for meaning and purpose. We want to be significant and for our lives to count. We want the world to be different as a result of our having been here. We have a need to create and to know why we are here. Science helps provide us with some answers about our physical world, but it cannot answer our deepest questions. What gives life meaning? What's our purpose? Who are we? Who will we become? What should we do with our lives? These are questions for religion. This is why we need science and faith. There are questions only science can answer, and there are questions only faith can answer. The Bible deals with life's deepest questions. The book of Ecclesiastes is all about the search for meaning. The writer begins expressing what a lot of us feel, "Meaningless, meaningless, everything is meaningless. Everything is chasing after wind." He finds that chasing money, power, and sex still leaves him empty. A life focused on himself still leaves him empty. Jesus taught his disciples in Matthew 10:39, "When you lose your life, you find it." Meaning comes as we give our lives away in service to something greater than ourselves. What gives your life meaning?

Affirmation: My life has meaning.
Prayer: God, give me a cause to live for that is bigger than myself.

Day 6 - What Defines You?

Pick three words that best characterize you. You might say funny, female, Texan, or bi-racial, musical, Christian. Choose any three words that best

63

define who you are. What are they? Then, if you had to choose two words out of those three words that best characterize you, which two words would you choose. Now, if you had to choose one word out of the remaining two words, which word would you choose? What one word best defines you? Is it where you are from (Texan)? Is it part of your biology (female)? Is it part of your personality (funny)? Is it your cultural heritage (bi-racial)? Is it related to your gifts or talents (musical)? Is it your relationship to others (son)? Or, does it represent your faith (Christian)? This simple exercise shows what you value. It shows you what most defines you as a person. How do you feel about what you chose? Would you change it? Was it hard to limit yourself to just one label? We are so much more than one thing, but we often put others and ourselves into categories. We think: he's smart, she's cool, he's poor, she's weird. In Jesus' day, lepers were labeled "unclean." That was the one word society used to define them. Because of their leprosy, people would not socialize with them or take time to get to know them. That is, except for Jesus. Jesus took time to talk with lepers who society discarded. Jesus knew there was more to them than one label. There is so much more to all of us. No one likes to be stereotyped or labeled. Take time to get to know others beyond the labels society puts on them. Don't let yourself or others be defined by a label.

Affirmation: I am not defined by one aspect of my life.
Prayer: God, help me not put labels on other people.

Day 7 - Chance or Destiny

Do you believe in chance or do you believe you control your own destiny? Some people see themselves as victims of whatever happens to them; they just accept that life has to be bad and have a fatalistic view of life; they may think that nothing will change so why even bother trying? Things will always be the way they are. Others believe that they control their own destiny; they believe the future is what they make it and that change is possible. They also know they can change the world. Ishmael had a choice. He had to choose between giving up on life after being rejected and making the most of the life he had. The truth is, there will be struggles for those who have it good, and there will be opportunities for those who have it bad. If you look for the negative you will find it; and if you look for the positive you will find it, too. Your success really depends more on how you see things than it does on your actual situation. Instead of focusing on what you don't have, focus on what you do have. Focus on who you are, not who you aren't. There are negative forces at work in the world, but it's up to you whether you give them power over your life. There are people who believe in chance and those who believe they control their own destiny. Which one are you?

Affirmation: I control my own destiny.
Prayer: Lord, help me focus on what I do have rather than on what I don't have.

Day 8 - Know Thyself

The great philosopher Socrates said, "Know thyself." It is a challenge to take the time to get to know who we are as individuals. We are all human beings and we share things in common with every other human being. We all eat, sleep, breathe, cry, and go to the bathroom. We are also part of a family and culture. There are things about us that we share in common with certain groups of people. We might share certain values, traditions, food, and music preferences with groups of people we are close with. But we are also individuals, and there are things about us that are unique to us. We may have different gifts, thoughts, or desires than those in our family, culture, or larger human family. We are part of the story of human history, but our story is unique. No one else exactly like us has ever lived, and no one else like us will come along again. You only have one life and one body, so you might as well get comfortable in your skin. Get to know yourself. You are the only you there is. You are the only you that will ever be!

Affirmation: I am unique. There is no one else like me.
Prayer: God, help me know myself.

Day 9 - Low Self-Esteem

I wouldn't be surprised if Ishmael had low self-esteem. When your step-brother gets all the attention, and you are overlooked, it would be hard to have a good self-image. Ishmael probably felt unwanted. It's hard to have healthy self-esteem when no one acknowledges your worth. But even when no one paid attention to Ishmael, God was there. God gave Ishmael a promise that he had an important future. Ishmael had to trust God's word in the absence of positive words from his family. God's promise gave Ishmael confidence and self-esteem. He was not forgotten, unwanted, or rejected. God was looking out for him. You may feel overlooked. You may be insecure and have low self-esteem, but you are esteemed by God. Believe what God has to say about you. God knows you by name. Matthew 10:30 says, "Every hair on your head is counted." God notices you. You have great worth.

Affirmation: I have incredible worth.
Prayer: Lord, in my lowest moments, help me remember how much You love me.

Day 10 - Overcoming Abuse

Abuse is damaging, no matter what form it comes in. There are different types of abuse that we might face in life. Physical abuse is when someone hits, punches, kicks, or injures you physically. Physical violence against children or in close relationships can be terrifying. Verbal abuse is when someone speaks hurtful and damaging words over you, when someone (family member, girl or boyfriend) tears you down with their words. Just because the words don't leave physical bruises doesn't mean they don't leave a mark. Verbal abuse can be harder to recognize than physical abuse, but it's still abuse. Sexual abuse is another type of abuse that is rampant in our world. Even in the church, abuse happens. Overall, one in four women and one in six men experience sexual abuse or sexual violence in their lifetime. When people experience abuse, they often feel guilt or shame, even though they didn't do anything to deserve it. No one deserves abuse or violence. When people experience abuse, they often feel like they have to keep silent about it. Sometimes someone tells them to not tell anyone what happened, or sometimes they're too embarrassed to tell anyone. If you have experienced abuse, you are not alone. Seek help from someone you can trust and talk with about what happened, or call 1-800-799-SAFE to talk with someone who can help.

Affirmation: I deserve to be free from abuse.
Prayer: God, help those who are suffering from abuse to find support and healing.

Day 11 - Healthy Relationships

Ishmael's story shows us how unhealthy relationships between adults can have a negative impact on their child. The decisions and actions of our parents can impact how we feel about ourselves and even influence how we treat other people later in our lives. Because of the bad relationship between his mother and father, it would have been easy for Ishmael to not trust people who wanted to be close to him out of fear that they might hurt him the way his father hurt his mother. God wants us to have healthy trusting relationships. Healthy relationships require courage, the courage to let people into our lives and allow them to love us the way that we deserve to be loved at the risk of being hurt. Sometimes creating healthy relationships requires reminding yourself that you deserve to be happy and to have healthy relationships in your life. You have to remind yourself that even though you may have been hurt by the mistakes of parents, you can write your own story. You deserve to be happy and you deserve to be loved. When God is at the center of your relationships, you can make it through, even when things get tough.

Affirmation: I can have healthy relationships. I deserve healthy relationships.
Prayer: Lord, help me keep You at the center of all my relationships.

Day 12 - Facing Bullies

Almost all youth experience being bullied at some point in their lives. Whether it's being bullied at school or online, bullying is happening more and more. Bullies thrive on power and use physical force and words to overpower others. One of the biggest bullies of the Bible was Goliath. He was larger, stronger, and meaner than any bully we will face. David was small, but smart, and he understood that Goliath had power; but David was not afraid. Goliath's power was that he could intimidate and instill fear in others. When David stood up to Goliath, it changed the game. Bullies want to make us feel small and powerless. They count on us not telling anyone, so we feel isolated. But there is strength in numbers. When we reach out to others -- parents, teachers, friends, and guidance counselors -- we can find help to stop the bullying. The best way to end mistreatment is to tell an adult so they can bring an end to it right away. Bullies are really insecure and often torment others in order to fit in. Maybe they are even bullied at home by a parent. When we understand the power dynamics of bullies, we do not have to fear or feel powerless.

Affirmation: I am not powerless.
Prayer: Lord, I pray for those who are bullied to not be afraid, and for those who bully to come to know You.

Day 13 - Causes and Symptoms

There is a story about a village near a river. Every day, bloody bodies would wash up on the river's edge. Day after day the people of the village would take the wounded people out of the river and care for them. Finally, one of the villagers asked, "What is causing all these wounded bodies to wash up on the river's edge? Why don't we look upstream to see who is throwing them in the river?" A lot of times we deal with the symptoms of problems, without looking at the causes. We might see a homeless person who is hungry, so we buy them a meal. We deal with the symptom: that they are hungry. But, to deal with the cause means we have to ask why they are homeless in the first place. Many homeless people struggle with mental illness and need treatment; and many cannot find employment, which means they cannot afford rent. A quarter of all homeless people has served in the military and may suffer from Post-Traumatic Stress Disorder (PTSD). A high percentage of homeless women and children are homeless because they are victims of domestic violence. They have to choose between being beaten at home and being homeless on the streets. When we start looking at the cause, we gain more empathy and begin to see that it will take more work on our part to address the root causes of homelessness. When you see a problem, identify the symptoms, but make sure you also go upstream and figure out the cause. We are called to not only do works of charity, but to seek justice. This requires caring for individuals who suffer, but to also address the larger systems -- economic and social -- that create the injustice. "Is this not the kind of fasting I have chosen: to loose the chains of injustice and untie the cords of the yoke, to set the oppressed free and break every yoke? (Isaiah 58:6)"

Affirmation: I can make an impact in someone else's life.
Prayer: Lord, I pray for those who are homeless today to find food and shelter, and I also pray that we can work toward ending the causes of homelessness in our country.

Day 14 - Resisting Drugs and Alcohol

Drugs are rampant in our society. Whether you live in the suburbs or the city, drugs are a big problem. In some states, marijuana has become legalized. In other states, you can face prison time for even possessing marijuana. Drugs can lead us down a dangerous path. Selling drugs can seem like an easy way to make money, but the consequences are very costly. Like Abraham, we want to bypass God's way to make our own path. The legal age for consuming alcohol in many U.S. states is twenty-one, but many experiment with underage drinking. When youth get impatient and drink before it's legal, they end up risking their own life and the lives of others. Alcohol affects underage drinkers more heavily than adults, which is one reason there is an age requirement. It can be hard to resist peer pressure and say no to temptation. Be patient. Don't rush to become an adult. Enjoy being young. I avoided drugs and alcohol, which allowed me to have a clear head. I didn't make the mistakes a lot of my friends made. Keep your focus on God. "Do not get drunk with wine because that will ruin your life. Instead, be filled with the Holy Spirit" (Ephesians 5:18).

Affirmation: I will not give into peer pressure.
Prayer: Lord, help me resist temptation and keep my focus on You.

Day 15 - Giving up Control

Eating disorders and cutting are symptoms of a deeper cause. Often it's a coping mechanism for something happening in someone's life that makes them feel out of control. I had family members who struggled with their weight, which caused me to worry about my weight, too. I would not eat to compensate for my family members' eating. I had to learn to be healthy for myself rather than act in response to someone else to feel in control. We have to talk through the pain and the causes that may be under the surface. Counseling gives us strategies for dealing with eating disorders and cutting. We can find freedom when we learn to let go of things we can't control. We can make our own choices regardless of what choices others make around us. You are beautiful as you are. You do not need to look, dress, talk, or act like anyone else. You do not have to fear; God is present to help you in your struggle. "Trust in the Lord with all your heart, and do not lean on your own understanding. In all your ways acknowledge him, and he will make straight your paths" (Proverbs 3:5-6).

Affirmation: I am Beautiful as I am.
Prayer: Lord, be my rock. I put my trust in You.

Day 16 - Let's Talk About Sex

There is a lot of sex in the Bible and many of the stories about sex are actually lessons in what not to do. The story of Abraham and Hager is one of them. Instead of waiting for God's timing, Abraham engages in sex outside of the marriage covenant. Like Abraham, you might have discovered it's difficult to wait to have sex. It's especially difficult when we see sex being treated so casually in our society. The reality is, there is a lot of sexual brokenness in the world. Not just in the world, but in the church as well. We don't talk about it much, but we all experience sexual brokenness. Pornography, sexual relationships outside of marriage, and sexual abuse are realities in this broken world. Sex sells, so advertisers use sexual images to get our attention. Bodies are airbrushed on magazines, giving us unrealistic views of women and men's bodies. God desires that we have a healthy sexuality. God created sex, so it is good; but it is meant to be within a covenant relationship. Song of Solomon 8:4 says, "Do not arouse or awaken love before its time." The best way to guard your heart is to wait until the person you are with is committed to you for life. If you have made mistakes in the past, you can be restored. King David struggled sexually and ended up sleeping with someone else's wife. (See, another lesson in what not to do!) David returned to the Lord with true repentance and God restored him. David had to live with the consequences of his actions but he was forgiven. David wrote Psalm 51 after he had messed up. It's a good prayer for us as we seek restoration in our lives: "Create in me a pure heart, O God, and renew a right spirit within me."

Affirmation: My past can be restored.
Prayer: Create in me a clean heart, O God.

Day 17 - Understanding Suicide

When someone takes his or her own life, it is a tragedy. If you know someone who has committed suicide you realize how devastating it can be for friends and family. In the past, people used to teach that those who commit suicide go to Hell; I think this is very destructive teaching. First of all, no one knows the eternal state of anyone else so it's best not to speculate. What we do know is: God is merciful. scripture says, "God's mercy will triumph over his judgment" (James 2:13). In the case of suicide, we can appeal to God's mercy. Secondly, we know now that the majority of people who commit suicide suffer from some form of mental health issue. For many, suicide is not simply about making a personal choice, but rather it's about battling a mental condition that is outside their control. People who struggle with suicidal thoughts do not need our judgment; they need support, counseling, and often medication. I know many youth struggle with suicidal thoughts, and may wonder if the world would be better without them. They might develop self-hatred and encounter feelings of worthlessness; or they may suffer heartache and heartbreak, and think they just want to die. But there's so much to live for. Whatever pain you are feeling now will pass and you will smile again. Old wounds do mend. If you have thoughts that are too overwhelming, reach out to someone right away. You are not alone. Ishmael probably wanted to end his life, but it was just the beginning. Your life is just beginning as well. The best is yet to come.

Affirmation: I have so much to live for.
Prayer: Why so downcast O my soul? I must put my hope in God.

Day 18 - Setting a New Course

I work for Mission Year, a program for 18-29 year olds who want to make an impact with their lives. Many of those who serve in our program have gone through a lot of challenges in their lives, but they want to set a new course. They don't want to be defined by their past or by their sorrow, so they commit a year to seeking God in the city. They live in community with a team of other Christians and become part of the life of an urban neighborhood. They build transforming relationships, and serve the needs of the community. It is life-changing for them and those they meet in the city. Some of them aren't sure they are fit to serve God. They think something in their past disqualifies them. But remember Paul -- he killed Christians. He was a murderer, but God used him to become one of the greatest missionaries of all time. Paul would say he was the worst of all sinners. But, if God could use him, then God can use anybody. It's never too late to set a new course. You can start today. "Here is a trustworthy saying that deserves full acceptance: Christ Jesus came into the world to save sinners—of whom I am the worst" 1 Timothy 1:15.

Affirmation: I can set a new course for my life.
Prayer: God, I give myself away so You can use me.

Day 19 - The Heart of the Father

Jesus referred to God as Father. The Greek word Jesus used was "Abba", which translates into "Daddy." Jesus used a word for God that was an intimate and affectionate term. Jesus' father Joseph is not mentioned in the Gospels after Jesus was born. If your father was absent or distant, it might take a while to understand that God is a different kind of father than what you experienced. God the Father loves you. Not only that, God likes you. God wants to be a close companion. God wants to fill the void in your heart and show you love, even if your earthly father was not present. Jesus said, "Which of you, if your son asks for bread, will give him a stone? Or if he asks for a fish, will give him a snake? If you, then, though you are evil, know how to give good gifts to your children, how much more will your Father in Heaven give good gifts to those who ask him (Matthew 7:9-11)."

Affirmation: I am loved by my heavenly Father.
Prayer: Father God, help me relate to You as a loving Father **and to know that You will always be there for me.**

Day 20 - The Mother Heart of God

Although we often talk about God as Father, there are images of the mother heart of God in scripture, too. In Luke 15, Jesus compared God to a woman looking for a lost coin. God is deeply concerned about us when we get lost and fall away from him. Isaiah 66:13 says, "As a mother comforts a child, so will I comfort you." In this passage, God is portrayed as a nurturing mother. This should not surprise us. The Bible says God created us male and female, in the image of God. This means God contains both masculine and feminine qualities. Men and women individually reflect God in different ways. If we only highlight the masculine aspects of God, we will miss out on a big part of who God is. When we embrace the masculine and feminine characteristics of God, we see that God is our helper in times of trouble, a rock and fortress, a loving father, and a nurturing mother. Ideally, our earthly parents are supposed to reflect the love of God to us, but in reality, they are imperfect. However, God's love is perfect. Even when our parents fail, which they will do, God is there to show us love unconditionally. Is it easier or harder for you to think of God as mother?

Affirmation: I can know God as a nurturing mother.
Prayer: God, help me to know You as a loving father and a nurturing mother.

Day 21 - As Is

One of my favorite things to do when I shop at a store is to look through the clearance section. I like getting things on sale and finding a good deal. In a clearance section, you will often see stickers that say, "As is." This means you can purchase the items at a big discount if you are willing to take them as they are. The items might be chipped or missing pieces, but a lot of times they are still in good shape even though there might be minor damages. Sometimes we might feel like damaged goods and wonder if anyone can ever love us. We worry that our imperfections are too much for anyone to take. In Romans, Paul says God loved us as is. "But God demonstrated his own love for us in this: while we were still sinners Christ died for us" (Romans 5:8). God showed us love in our lowest, dirtiest, and darkest state. God saw our worst and still loved us. While we were enemies of God, God chose to lavish us with love and send Christ to die in our place. We are loved unconditionally. We are loved "as is."

Affirmation: I am loved as I am.
Prayer: Lord, help me know Your unconditional love in my head and in my heart.

Day 22 - Fear Factor

There used to be a show on television called "Fear Factor." Contestants would compete by facing their worst fears. They would be challenged to eat disgusting things or lay down in a box full of scorpions, rats, or spiders. If you were afraid of heights, you were out of luck because you often had to do a death-defying stunt elevated in the air. Fear is a strange thing and is mostly in our heads. I've known people who were afraid of bridges so they never left their state. Fear can keep us from experiencing God's abundant life and fear can keep us from taking action. I felt called to live and work with Mission Year on the west side of Chicago, but I also had to overcome fears. I had heard a lot about violence and crime in Chicago, so during the first few months there, I bottled a lot of anxiety. One of my neighbors reminded me of a scripture verse that helped them face their own fears. It's 2 Timothy 1:7: "God has not given us a spirit of fear, but of love, power, and a sound mind." This helped me remember that the God I serve is greater than any challenges I might face. Faith helps us overcome fear so we can experience abundant life.

Affirmation: I will not fear.
Prayer: Lord, give me courage to face my fears and overcome them with faith.

Day 23 - Leadership Lessons: It's Not How You Start...

I ran track in high school. During one home meet, I really wanted to impress my family and friends who showed up to watch me run the 400-meter race. When the gun went off, I took off, sprinting out of the gate. I heard shouts from my friends. I was out front. I was imagining myself crossing the finish line. I was in the lead for the first 100 meters and was still in the lead after 200 meters. At the three-fourths mark, I completely ran out of gas; everyone passed by and I ended up in last place. I learned an important lesson: it's not how you start that's important, it's how you finish. There are a lot of biblical examples of people who started well in life and leadership, but ended poorly. David had a great start. He defeated Goliath and became King of Israel, but he ended up committing adultery with Bathsheba and sending her husband to die in battle. Many of the kings of Israel had great starts but ended up doing wrong in the eyes of the Lord. It's not enough to start well. We have to finish what we start. Have you ever quit something you started? It takes discipline and patience to see things through. Don't just start well. Finish strong! "Being confident in this, that He who began a good work in you will carry it on to completion until the day of Christ Jesus" (Philippians 1:6).

Affirmation: I can finish what I start.
Prayer: God, help me finish strong in life and in the goals I set for myself.

Day 24 - Leadership Lessons: It's How You Finish

Not everyone has a good start. There are a lot of biblical stories of people who had bad starts but ended up finishing well. Moses, Paul, and Ishmael all had bad starts; but each of them put their lives in God's hand and saw their lives redeemed. You might have had a rough start; you may have done something you aren't proud of. You may have had something done to you. Just because you have a bad start doesn't mean you can't finish well. Paul was responsible for putting many Christians to death before his conversion. He had a really bad start, but he spent the rest of his life telling people about Christ, and ended up losing his life for his faith. He was killed in much the same way he had killed other Christians. Before he died, he wrote these words in 2 Timothy 4:7: "I have fought the good fight. I have finished the race. I have kept the faith." He may have started bad, but he made sure he finished the race well. That is our job in leadership and in life. We are not expected to be perfect, but we are expected to finish the race. You will stumble, and you will fall, but don't beat yourself up; don't stay on the ground. Get up and keep running the race. Remember, it's not how you start . . . it's how you finish that matters.

Affirmation: I will finish the race.
Prayer: Lord, give me the endurance to run the race to the end.

Day 25 - YOLO

"YOLO," which stands for "You only live once," became a popular expression and hash tag a couple years ago. In a positive sense, this means to take courageous action and live life to the fullest. There is truth in the statement. We do only live once. We only get one chance to live on this earth, which begs the question, how do you want to be remembered? What do you want your tombstone to say about you? What do you want your legacy to be? Growing up, I was taught to leave things better than I found them. If I stayed at someone's house, I needed to make sure I cleaned up after myself and even left things in better shape than when I arrived. I think this is how we should live life. We should strive to leave the world better than we found it. The Iroquois tribe had a practice of thinking how their decisions today would impact seven generations (140 years later) into the future. They didn't just think about what they wanted for themselves in the moment, but they also took time to measure the impact of their actions on future generations. We only live once on this earth. We can take that for granted or we can use our time to make a positive impact on others. We need to think about how our actions will make life better or worse for future generations. At the end of our life, will we be able to say we left the world better than we found it? Did we use our time to make life better for others? How do you want to be remembered?

Affirmation: I only live once. I will make it count.
Prayer: Lord, help me to leave the world better than I found it.

Day 26 - Stand by Me

Ishmael represents those who experience injustice, those who are excluded and outcast. In this story, God chooses to stand with Ishmael when no one else will. Throughout scripture, God stands with those who are poor, outcast, and oppressed. Not only that, the Bible calls us to stand with them too. The prophet Micah says, "You know what the Lord requires of you, but to do justly, love mercy, and walk humbly with your God (Micah 6:8)." If we are to walk humbly with God, we have to go to the places God goes. God is always going to the margins of society where people are experiencing injustice. We see this in the life of Jesus. He goes to the blind, the lepers, the tax collectors, and the sinners. In Matthew 25, Jesus says, "What you did for the least of these (the homeless, the hungry, the prisoner, the sick, and the stranger), you did for me." When we stand with the marginalized, we stand with Christ. Jesus is asking us to stand with him. How can you get closer to those who are on the margins? Are you willing to stand with Jesus by standing with those who are outcast? We have an opportunity to be a light in someone's darkness.

Affirmation: I can be a light in someone else's darkness.
Prayer: Lord, give me courage to stand with those no one else will stand with.

Day 27 - God Pays Attention to the Needy

God is attuned to the needy and has a special heart for those who are in need of protection. God cares for the widows, orphans, and economically vulnerable. Many in our country are on the edge of poverty, and there are families who are one paycheck away from being homeless. Many people suffer from food insecurity, which means they do not know where their next meal is coming from. A lot of people look down on those who are poor rather than have compassion on them. But, God pays attention to the poor and cares for them. A lot of times the poor are invisible in our society. We do not see them. We ignore them. First John 3:16-17 challenges us to pay attention to the poor. "If anyone has enough money to live well and sees a brother or sister in need but has no pity on them, how can the love of God be in that person? Dear children, let us not love with words or speech, but with actions and truth."

Affirmation: I will show compassion to those in need.
Prayer: God, help me pay attention to those who are poor and in need.

Day 28 - Forgiving Your Parents

Ishmael's parents were not perfect. Chances are, your parents are not perfect either. The truth is, there are no perfect parents. Even Christian parents make mistakes. Just because someone's parents go to church or read the Bible, it doesn't mean they don't have struggles. Christian parents get stressed and angry, too. Stress can even be displayed on the way to attending church. Being a Christian doesn't mean you are perfect, it means you are able to admit when you mess up; and you seek to make things right. Although my parents were strong Christians, they made mistakes. One thing that really had an impact on me was when my parents would come to my sister and me and ask for forgiveness when they had made a mistake or acted out of anger. It allowed me to realize my parents were human and struggled like everyone else. I had to learn to forgive my parents. Parenting is a huge responsibility and it certainly isn't easy. Parents do the best they can, and sometimes, parents may not know how to parent. It could be because they didn't have the best examples of healthy parenting when they were growing up. No matter how good parents may be, they will ultimately make mistakes and need our forgiveness. Forgiveness frees us from bitterness and resentment, and brings healing for them and us. Colossians 3:13 states, "Bear with each other and forgive whatever grievances you may have against one another. Forgive as the Lord forgave you." Have your parents ever asked for your forgiveness when they made a mistake? Have you forgiven your parents for not being perfect? Have you ever told them you forgive them?

Affirmation: I am free when I forgive.
Prayer: Lord, help me forgive my parents for mistakes they have made.

Day 29 - A Greater Purpose

We all have greatness within; we just need to tap into it; no one is insignificant. Martin Luther King Jr. said, "Everyone can be great, because everyone can serve." Jesus said, "The one who wants to be greatest, must become the servant of all (Matthew 20:26)." When we serve our fellow brothers and sisters, especially those in need, we tap into our greatness. Greatness is our capacity to love one another and our willingness to do something for another without seeking something in return. Greatness is demonstrated through small, consistent acts of love. Greatness is committing to let go of anger and forgiving others. Greatness is lifting up someone who has fallen down. Greatness is refusing to stay down when we have fallen. Greatness is insisting that everyone be treated as a child of God. Greatness is giving and receiving love. Greatness is the act of giving of ourselves for the greater good of others. Let's pursue this kind of greatness!

Affirmation: I can achieve greatness.
Prayer: God, help me seek greatness through service.

Day 30 - You Made It

One of my favorite praise songs is "Never would have made it," by Marvin Sapp. The chorus goes, "Never would have made it. Never could have made it without you. I would have lost it all. But now I see you were there for me." The song reminds me of what God has brought me through. I am reminded I could not have done it on my own. Luckily, we do not have to go through life on our own; Christ is with us. More than that, scripture says, Christ is *in* us (Colossians 1:27). Jesus said, "The kingdom of God is within you" (Luke 17:21). You have extra resources to handle whatever it is you face. God's Spirit is inside of you. You can endure because Christ lives within you. You can have hope in dark times because Christ is in you. You can make it through the toughest battles because Christ lives in you. We have all made it through something. We all have a testimony to share. What have you made it through? Tell someone today what Christ has brought you through.

Affirmation: Christ is in me.
Prayer: Christ, help me make it through whatever challenges I might face.

CHAPTER FIVE
- HAGAR -

KATHY KHANG

Day 1 - Even When You Are Alone, God Hears You

Hagar was a slave and a single mother. In so many respects, Hagar was alone. She did not have a family, even though she became a mother, most likely due to a situation she did not choose. She did not have her own home or her own name, because as a slave, she was property that belonged to her owner, Sarah. Hagar was alone, and the image of her alone in the wilderness sobbing for fear of losing what she had left – her own life and that of her son's -- isn't too far off, perhaps, from the hopelessness and fear you have experienced in your own life. The only hope in Hagar's story is God. The father of her child failed her. Her owner failed her. But even when it looks like there is no hope, God hears Hagar's son crying and sends an angel to comfort her. Even when Hagar thought she was alone, she wasn't. She never was.

Affirmation: Even in the worst circumstances, when everyone and everything has failed me, I am not alone.
Prayer: God, help me to know that even when life seems completely hopeless, I am not alone.

Day 2 - Hearing Angels

Hagar's story is challenging for me because I'm not sure what to do about angels. I've met people who have become angels to me – friends who have provided a much-needed word of comfort or support, or financial help when things looked impossible. I don't know if that is what it means when we read an angel of God called out to Hagar; that someone wandering in the desert suddenly heard a baby's cry. But I know that a voice reminding Hagar to have hope is what snapped her out of her grief. Whether or not it was a Hollywood version of an angel, or something we can't understand unless it happens to us, Hagar heard hope. She heard God through an angel telling her, "Do not be afraid."

Affirmation: When we know God, we do not need to be afraid.

Prayer: Lord, help me hear the angels who remind me to not be afraid, and help me to be that angel to others.

Day 3 - You Can't See What You Can't See

Hagar couldn't see any hope. She had been kicked out of the only community she had been a part of, with only some food and water. And when that ran out, she couldn't see any other way out. Could you? The problem is that she had forgotten what another angel of God had already told her – Hagar was going to have so many descendants that there would be too many to count. In that time, talk of descendants meant a future because you would have children, which meant you would live to see more than just another day. Hagar couldn't find any hope because she was focused on the moment (which was a pretty harsh moment), and she lost the big picture. She couldn't see the water until the angel pointed it out. Hagar also couldn't understand that her hope shouldn't rest in a single moment of the present.

Affirmation: My present circumstances are not the full picture.
Prayer: God, help me to see beyond the limitations of my present to possibility of my future.

Day 4 - What Hagar's Story Is Not

Hagar's full story is tricky. Hagar is a slave. She runs away because her mistress has mistreated her, and then she is told by an angel of God to go back to her owner and submit (Genesis 16). This sounds like the Bible is telling you or someone you love to go back and stay in an abusive relationship. It is not. For whatever reason, the angel of God told Hagar to go back, but that is not the moral of the story. No one -- not a pastor, or a respected youth leader, or a mentor -- should use that point out of context to tell someone to stay in an abusive relationship. If we broke up every story in the Bible and took them out of context we might find ways to justify slavery, cheating, and murder, but that is not what God invites us into. Hagar's whole story is one of God's provision, safety, and redemption.

Affirmation: God isn't a God of abuse and pain, but one of hope and redemption.
Prayer: For those in abusive relationships, I pray for hope. May I be the hands and feet for those who need hope.

Day 5 - When Freedom Comes Unexpectedly

What Abraham does to Hagar sounds horrible. He kicks her out with some food and water and sends her and their son, Ishmael, into the wilderness. I don't know about you, but I do not like being out in the wilderness. I don't even like camping. The thought of getting kicked out frightens me, though it may have already happened to you. But for Hagar, because she was a slave owned by Abraham and Sarah, it was actually the only way she could become free. It actually makes me think about an ex-boyfriend: the one who pushed me to the ground so hard that I needed to go to the hospital; the one who accused me of flirting and cheating, when I was doing no such thing. He broke up with me, and I thought my world was over. What I didn't immediately understand was that I was finally free.

Affirmation: Sometimes the only way we can find freedom from brokenness and hopelessness is to have it forced on us in unexpected ways.
Prayer: God, free me from the relationships and situations that are keeping me from your plan for me.

Day 6 - Falling Out of Favor

Sarah's relationship with Hagar is messed up – slave owner and slave. Sarah uses Hagar to get something she wants and then kicks her out. At the heart of it is an example of envy, competition, and jealousy, and I'm guilty of all those things. How many times have you or I looked at someone else's life and wanted what she or he has? How many times have you or I tried to take or get something that isn't yours or mine to have? I can easily paint Sarah as a pretty awful woman, until I take a look at my own heart.

Affirmation: We need to look at everyone in Hagar's story because there are many lessons to be learned.
Prayer: God, don't let me only see myself as the hero or heroine; help me to see myself in the very human people in Hagar's story.

Day 7 - Once God Speaks, Listen

Sometimes I like to wallow in my own stuff, to hear my own whining. Of course, at the time I don't necessarily see it as whining. I see it as letting off steam. Hagar was doing more than letting off steam when she cried; she was scared her son was going to die of dehydration. But what happened after is the key for Hagar and for any of us caught in retelling our bad-situation story to others. Hagar hears the angel of God tell her to let go of her fear and to take her son by the hand. Her eyes are opened and she sees a well of water. Does she sit back down and start crying about what has happened and what she was afraid of? No. Once God speaks, Hagar gets up and gets her son a drink of water.

Affirmation: Living into God's promises sometimes requires us to simply listen and get up.
Prayer: God, thank You for being there to provide what I cannot see. Help me to listen, to see, and to get up.

Day 8 - Who Determines Your Future?

When I started school I couldn't speak English. Because of this, I'm sure I had a teacher or two who wondered if I could succeed in school, let alone in life. If I had listened to them I'm sure my heart would've sunk, but fortunately I didn't understand them! Sarah spoke hurtful words when she announced that the slave woman and her son would neither have a place in her family, nor would they have a future. Hagar was that slave woman, and she might not have heard the words that Sarah said to her, but she lived the consequences: she and her young son were kicked out of the only home they knew, with nothing but some food and water. Hagar cried out in hopelessness because she had forgotten that Sarah wasn't the one determining her future but that God was in control.

Affirmation: Even when other people beat me down with words or even actions, God ultimately is the one in control. I must look to God.
Prayer: God, remind me that You are in control and You alone are my future.

Day 9 - She's Your Mother?

Ishmael goes on to marry and have twelve sons of his own. God is faithful and follows through on His promises to Hagar and Ishmael. But before Ishmael's marriage and the birth of his twelve sons, I imagine there weren't many people thinking he and his mother were going to amount to much. In fact, Hagar, being a slave girl, probably didn't come to the mind of many people unless they needed her to do some work. But that's the crazy thing about God. He doesn't care if you are the child of a single parent. He doesn't care if you're a single parent. He loves you and He has a plan for you!

Affirmation: God doesn't judge me before He loves me.
Prayer: God, thank You for loving me even when people can't seem to see past my circumstances.

Day 10 - Everyone Makes Mistakes

Abraham is stuck between a rock and a hard place. He considers Ishmael his son even though he and Ishmael's mother are not married. Abraham wants to do right by his wife and son, but clearly this situation is not working out for anyone. The Bible doesn't tell us whether or not Abraham sought God out, but it is clear that God told Abraham that despite what Sarah, his wife, was suggesting – getting rid of Hagar and their son Ishmael, which could lead to danger or death for both of them – Abraham did not need to be so worried. Imagine how distressed Abraham would have been at the thought of kicking Hagar and Ishmael out of their home, and then in addition, told not to worry. That's God. Even in the worst situations, God reminded Abraham that God alone is in control.

Affirmation: God doesn't have to imagine my worst-case scenario. He knows where I am right now.
Prayer: God, give me the faith to believe You are in control, and I have nothing to worry about.

Day 11 - Everyone Makes Mistakes, II

Sarah is another one in Hagar's story I just can't figure out. Described as being past the childbearing age, she eventually does the very thing God had promised in Genesis 18: she gives birth to a son. I don't know about you, but I would like to think that if I knew God had promised me something that crazy and delivered on the promise, I would be too busy and too ecstatic to care about a young boy mocking me. But that is what Sarah does. Instead of basking in the miracle of her son Isaac, she frets over Hagar's son (the one Hagar has given birth to because Sarah put her husband Abraham up to it). Sarah demands Abraham kick Hagar and Ishmael out. I would like to think Sarah regrets her decision at a later time, but we don't know that. We only know that God turns Sarah's pettiness into an opportunity to give Hagar the freedom she could not obtain by herself. Hagar now has a chance to be a free woman, even though freedom might not feel good at the moment.

Affirmation: God doesn't squander our lives even if we squander joyful moments.
Prayer: God, remind me to live in gratitude.

Day 12 - God's Blessing is Best

We don't know much more about Ishmael except that he went on to marry and have twelve sons. Even though Abraham was Ishmael's birth father, Ishmael never received a blessing from him. In that culture, the father would pass a word of blessing as well as an inheritance to all of his sons. Abraham did that for Isaac as well as the other sons he had with his concubines (Genesis 25:6). Ishmael was the only son who did not receive anything from Abraham. For some of us, an encouraging word from our earthly father means the world to us. For some of us, the lack of an earthly father has created a deep sense of loss or pain. Ishmael and Hagar's story reminds me that though our earthly relationships can be less than perfect, God's blessing is truly the one that lasts.

Affirmation: Friends and family are a blessing, but they are human. God's blessing and promises are the only ones I can always count on.
Prayer: Even when I hunger for the approval and love of people, thank You God for being the one to hear everything.

Day 13 - I Didn't Ask for This

Have you ever found yourself in a situation that you honestly, truly did not ask to be in? How did you get out of it? Hagar is in that kind of situation from the moment we meet her. She is a slave. Later she becomes pregnant by her owner. She is mistreated. She is kicked out and abandoned. There are some bad situations that we put ourselves into, but that is absolutely not the case with Hagar. And yet, over and over, we are reminded that God is there. He doesn't always save her from the circumstance in the way she may have hoped, but God is always there to remind Hagar that He knows what is going on, and that He has a plan and a purpose for her and her son.

Affirmation: I may not have asked to be in a particular situation, but God is always an option for me.
Prayer: God, help me, even when I feel stuck in an unfavorable circumstance.

84

Day 14 - What Name Would You Give God?

It has never crossed my mind to give God a name, but Hagar and her story make me think about it. In Genesis 16 we see Hagar pregnant and running away from Sarah. God's angel finds Hagar and tells her to go back. He tells her to return because God has a bigger purpose for her than sitting near a spring in the desert. God has a name for her son and describes his personality and his future. And then Hagar gives God a name, which is a powerful, symbolic gesture even in our current culture. She says, "You are the God who sees me."

Affirmation: I have a definite name for God
Prayer: God, help me to see You as part of my story as I am a part of Your story.

Day 15 - God Has Always Seen Us

When the angel of God paints a picture of the future for Hagar I am challenged and reminded that the God of the Old Testament is still the same God of the twenty-first century. The God who had a vision for Hagar -- a single mother with no home or means to a future of her own -- is the God you and I can interact with. Even if we haven't given God the time of day until this moment, Hagar's story reminds me that this doesn't matter. Hagar names God as "the God who sees me" because she recognizes that God had always been around. It was actually at that moment when she was acknowledging His presence when she says, "I have now seen the one who sees me." God was there all along.

Affirmation: It doesn't matter when I finally acknowledge God, because that doesn't stop God from being there for me.
Prayer: Thank you, God, for being the one who has always seen me.

Day 16 - God Isn't Afraid of the Mess

There are lots of things in the Bible that honestly make me wonder, "Why would God allow this?" Take for instance Hagar's story. She is a slave. She gets pregnant by her slave owner. The slave owner's wife mistreats her. We are spared the details, but when I think of a slave I don't think of a teen romance ending accidentally in a pregnancy. I think of slavery, rape, and abuse. Why would God allow this? On the other hand, I am a bit

85

relieved that the Bible, and ultimately God, isn't afraid to tackle real life situations that still happen today.

Affirmation: The Bible and God do not sugarcoat what happens in this world.
Prayer: God, help me to trust in You even when the world around me is crazy.

Day 17 - Where Are You Going?

When things get a little too complicated, difficult, frustrating, or confusing, I like to run away. Sometimes it's by procrastinating, avoiding, or ignoring. Sometimes I literally run – run down the street, around the block, up and down the stairs. More often than not, I don't know why I am running or where I am going until afterwards. When Hagar runs away from Sarah, she is on the move, but she doesn't know where she is going. How do we know this? The angel of God asks her, "...where have you come from, and where are you going?" Hagar only knows how to answer the first half of the question. God's angel gives Hagar the answer to the second half of the question.

Affirmation: God knows where I am going even when I do not.
Prayer: God, help me to stop running away and help me to listen to Your directions.

Day 18 - Who Gets an Angel

Hagar's story has a lot of angels, even angels who talk with Abraham and Sarah. The Bible is full of angels of God who appear at the perfect moment, and usually I imagine them to be not-quite human, floating just above the ground wearing white robes and glowing. But the important thing isn't what they look like or what they wear, but whom they speak to and what they say. Maybe you would expect God to send angels to talk to important people like Abraham or Sarah, but God sends angels to Hagar, the pregnant slave girl, who becomes the abandoned single mother. The angels speak words of comfort, encouragement, and direction. Who doesn't need an angel every now and then?

Affirmation: God doesn't just speak to important people. He speaks to ordinary people just like Hagar, and people just like me.
Prayer: God, thank You for including me in Your plans.

Day 19 - Angels Are Everywhere

While we are on the subject of angels, when was the last time an angel talked with you? If you are waiting for a not-quite human wearing a white robe appearing and disappearing, you might be waiting a while. In the meantime, take a moment and think about the people who are truly angels in your life, like the one who appeared to Hagar in her most desperate moments. The angel comforted Hagar when she was afraid, reminding her that God had not abandoned her or her son; God heard the crying and saw him lying under the bushes. The angel offered advice and direction and encouraged Hagar. Who are the real life angels who have come to you in those times of need, worry, and fear?

Affirmation: Angels aren't imaginary. God uses people every day to remind me that I am not alone.
Prayer: God, thank You for the angels you send to me, and let me be an angel to remind others You are with them.

Day 20 - God is Practical

Maybe I've watched too many movies, but when I think of ways to save Hagar and Ishmael from death, I imagine something more dramatic than a well. I imagine Hagar wanting revenge and some sort of triumphant return to the village to show Sarah up. But God doesn't need a bad movie to know exactly what Hagar and Ishmael need in order to survive. The Bible says God opened Hagar's eyes and right there she saw a well of water. Water. It makes total sense. Money or food often come to mind when I think of ways to "save" people from dying, but when you're in the desert, money isn't going to help and food may further dehydrate you. You need water.

Affirmation: God knows on a practical level exactly what I need.
Prayer: God, help me to trust You, especially when You provide exactly what I need, and not necessarily what I want.

Day 21 - Hagar, Water, and Jesus

It's easy to get stuck in a single story of the Bible and not see the whole picture. I love that God opens Hagar's eyes and there is a well of water where she can quench her son's thirst and then perhaps her own real thirst. God uses water many times in the Bible in different ways to provide for His people. Later in the Bible God parts the water -- the Red Sea --

to create a path of escape for His people. In the New Testament, Jesus approaches a woman at a well of water, and that conversation leads to the conversion of many in her community. Jesus turns water into wine when the host of a wedding is about to run out of wine for his guests. Water – real and symbolic – is a reminder of God's provision throughout time.

Affirmation: There is nothing too ordinary to remind us that God will provide for us.
Prayer: God, help me be thankful for the ordinary and extraordinary ways You provide for me.

Day 22 - Everyone Needs a Reminder

It was only in Genesis 16 that Hagar gives God a name recognizing God as the God who sees her. He was always the God who had always seen her, but it wasn't until then that she understood that. But by Genesis 21, she had forgotten God. She's back out on her own, this time with her son, and she has lost hope and direction just like the last time we saw her in the Bible. But, God doesn't punish her for forgetting. God doesn't slap her on the wrist. He reminds her that not only does He hear her son Ishmael crying, but He sees that she cannot hear him. The God who sees Hagar then opens her eyes so she can see again. Isn't that incredible? Not only can she see the well of water that God provided in the desert, but she can also see with her heart that God is with her still.

Affirmation: Our ability -- or inability -- to see God doesn't limit God from opening up our eyes and hearts.
Prayer: God, open my eyes so that I can see!

Day 23 - Love Is What We Need First

I don't know why Hagar sat apart from her son, the crying Ishmael. I know that when my kids were infants there were many nights when all I wanted to do was hold them and stare at their tiny, perfect features. But since then, there have been many times when their inconsolable cries have made me feel helpless, like nothing I could do or give was enough. Ishmael wasn't a tiny infant. He was most likely close to his teenage years, and Hagar was out of water. There was nothing else she could give him. Or was there? God tells her to lift Ishmael up out from under the bushes and to hold his hand. That's it. From then on God says

He's in control by telling her, "I will make him into a great nation." God will do some heavy lifting, but there is one thing you can and must do for your son or daughter: lift them up out of the bushes and hold them. In short, God reminds Hagar to love.

Affirmation: God provides for our physical and emotional needs.
Prayer: Help me trust You God to meet my needs instead of giving up.

Day 24 - We Are Not the Sacrifice

Something about the picture of Hagar coming to her senses and lifting Ishmael out of the bushes makes me think of Genesis 22 when Abraham is tested and asked to sacrifice his son Isaac. Just as Abraham is about to do the unthinkable and actually sacrifice Isaac, God stops him and shows him a ram caught in the bushes that he is to sacrifice instead. Hagar has all but given up hope, thinking that she will watch her son die, and just a chapter later we see Ishmael's father believing he will see his other son die as well. For both Hagar and Abraham, it takes God to give them hope when neither can see another option; God reminds both of them that their sons are not the sacrifice to accomplish God's will. God reminds both Hagar and Abraham that He is faithful and will provide.

Affirmation: God doesn't bring us to a low point to demand a sacrifice. He meets us where we are at to give us hope.
Prayer: Lord, show me what I cannot see. Give me hope when I cannot hope.

Day 25 - Sometimes There Are No Words

I don't always know what to say to God in prayer. I am comforted knowing that when Hagar hears God's angel call out to her by name she doesn't speak. What can you say when you think there is absolutely nothing left and you are afraid and exhausted? Common courtesy might expect Hagar to say a quick "Thank you" at the very least, but there is no expectation of that. God doesn't wait for Hagar to answer; He just opens her eyes.

Affirmation: A relationship with God is a two-way street, but God also knows that sometimes His love is powerful even in silence.
Prayer: Lord, today I cannot watch this dream or hope of mine die. Hear my cry.

Day 26 - God's Gift of Presence

Hagar wasn't promised riches for herself or for her son. She was told God heard her son's cries and that God would make her son into a great nation. Ishmael wouldn't be in the line of patriarchs of God's people, not like Isaac, Abraham's other son, would be. But after facing abandonment and death, "God was with the boy as he grew up" (Genesis 21:20 TNIV). As a reader, I am deeply comforted that it was important enough for us to be reminded that God gave Ishmael and Hagar the gift of His presence despite who they were or what they would become.

Affirmation: God doesn't care who I am, where I am, or what I am doing right now. God is with me.
Prayer: God, help me know how You are present in my life today.

Day 27 - Pick Your Own Adventure

Hagar's story reads a bit like a pick-your-own-adventure story where you, the reader, can choose different twists in the story to change the ending. When I read Hagar's story of an unwanted pregnancy I actually think, "If only Abraham had believed in God's promises and let people who might be affected by that promise in on the secret." What if Abraham had believed God when he was told in Genesis 15, 17, and 18 that he would have a son and what if Abraham had let his wife Sarah in on the promise? Could all of the drama with Hagar and Ishmael have been avoided? Maybe. But at the very least it makes me wonder how tight I hold God's love for people close to my heart without letting those around me in on the secret.

Affirmation: I shouldn't keep the secret of God's love, promises, and hope a secret from the people around me!
Prayer: God, give me the courage to believe, and to let people around me know about You!

Day 28 - Sarah and Hagar – How We Turn on Ourselves

Sarah and Hagar have a complicated relationship in a culture that reduced women to their ability to bear children, particularly sons. Sarah is not living up to cultural expectations when she fails to bear children, and when her plan to provide a surrogate succeeds; she punishes the woman who provided her husband with a son. When you find yourself hurt, what is your first instinct? For most of us, if we're brutally honest, it's to hurt someone in return, preferably the one who hurt us first.

Clearly, with Sarah and Hagar, their relationship never started out on equal footing: Sarah owned Hagar as a slave girl. However broken the relationship started, it was no excuse to continue hurting Hagar. Fortunately for everyone, God intervenes repeatedly to repair what can be repaired. Sarah has a biological son of her own. Her husband Abraham celebrates that son -- Isaac -- while still keeping a place in his heart for Ishmael. And ultimately God fulfills His promises despite Sarah and Abraham's attempts at "justice."

Affirmation: God isn't deterred by our brokenness; but we are surprised by His faithfulness.
Prayer: God, help me to deal with my anger and disappointment before I use it as a weapon against others.

Day 29 - Who Is God?

Hagar's story shows us God's character through an exchange of names. God tells Hagar to name her son Ishmael, which means "God hears." In turn, Hagar gives God the name "the God who sees." Isn't it interesting to read this passage in Genesis 16:11-13? God tells Hagar through an angel not only what He will do by giving Hagar a picture of her future and Ishmael's future, but He also fulfills it in His actions. God, the God who hears and sees, observes Hagar running from her owner, hears Hagar tell her story, and later opens Hagar's eyes.

Affirmation: God doesn't just sit up there in Heaven waiting for us to fail. He sees us, hears us, and opens our eyes!
Prayer: God, thank You for being a God who is with me!

Day 30 - You Don't Have to Know to Know

It is unclear whether or not Hagar actually knew it was God in the same way Abraham and Sarah would know God as Yahweh, because Hagar was an Egyptian slave. She most likely knew of the God her masters worshipped without necessarily "believing"; that is, until she ran away and had an interaction in the desert, which is repeated years later. She knows enough to know that the one who spoke to her, heard her and saw her, and that was enough for Hagar to obey. She didn't need to know everything to know that God had heard her and found her before she had everything figured out.

Affirmation: Just because I don't have a relationship with God right now doesn't mean God doesn't have a relationship with me.
Prayer: God, thank You for approaching me even before I knew who You really are.

CHAPTER SIX

- ESTHER -

SANDRA MARIA VAN OPSTAL

Day 1 - Who Am I?

Growing up as a second generation Latina shaped my definition of self. Moving from a racially diverse urban community to an affluent white suburb formed my identity as well. I had friends with tons of money and I'd studied in a public library that looked like a fancy hotel. If I can be honest with you, for most of my childhood, the only people who looked like me were subservient people; they were never the bosses. The way people talked about Latinos brought me a lot of shame. Living in this tension was too much for me. I fit in as best as I could, learning not only a new language, but also a whole new way of acting. As my faith in God grew, those identities crashed. I began to ask, "Who am I?" On this journey, I found that the story of Esther set me free to embrace my identity. Esther, a young exiled orphan, saves her people from annihilation. How, you ask? It is a drama about calling and courage. Read the story of Esther in one sitting. What questions, crisis, or events do you resonate with as you journey to discover your identity?

Affirmation: It is important to know our stories; they shape our identity.
Prayer: God, help me to see that You have been present throughout my journey.

Day 2 - What's in a Name?

Names are very important in scripture because they define you, literally. Names were a way for parents to speak promise into the lives of their children. Although some parents today are designing more creative names based on sound, many cultures today still follow this tradition, of naming children based upon their hopes for their children. Naming our son Justo Alejandro, meaning "just defender of mankind," is a way of hoping that our son will become someone who stands for justice. Therefore, whenever you find a name in scripture that is explained, pay attention. In Esther 2:7 we learn that the young woman Hadassah was also called Esther. She was given two names, one Jewish and one Persian. We find out that both her names suit her; Hadassah means courage while Esther means star. This was likely done so that she could navigate both worlds -- her Jewish ghetto as well as her Persian culture. Many of the ethnic minority young adults I work with have two names, a Korean and an American, or a Chinese and an American. Their parents, who wanted to ensure that they could navigate all of their worlds, gave their names to them. Maybe your parents did the same with you? Do you know anyone with two names? What is their story? What is the story behind your name? Your story, like Esther's, may include a journey of needing to navigate two worlds. How has that shaped you?

Affirmation: No matter what names or name our parents gave to us, God calls us beloved.
Prayer: Lord, help me to accept the names given to me as well as their stories as a part of my journey.

Day 3 - Listen Up

Much of Esther's success is based on the fact that she listened to her mentors. She was effective in part because she obeyed what Mordecai and Hegai advised her to do. We get some early clues that she is good at listening.

"Esther had not made known her people or kindred, for Mordecai had commanded her not to make it known. And every day Mordecai walked in front of the court of the harem to learn how Esther was and what was happening to her...When the young woman went in to the king in this way, she was given whatever she desired to take with her from the harem to the king's palace...She would not go in to the king again, unless the king delighted in her and she was summoned by name. When the turn came for Esther to go in to the king, she asked for nothing except what Hegai, the king's eunuch, who had charge of the women, advised. Now Esther was winning favor in the eyes of all who saw her" (Esther 2:10-11, 13, 15).

Esther could have felt like Mordecai was soft, or that Hegai was a hater who didn't want her to have nice stuff. She could have accused them of being "party poopers," but instead she listened. Esther took their advice because she knew that they had seen some things and been through some things, and that they had wisdom to offer.

How do you respond when mentors give you advice? Do you write them off because they are old or just "don't get it," or do you try to see where they are coming from?

Affirmation: Wisdom takes time to develop; I must take advantage of the wise mentors God has placed around me.
Prayer: God help me to not act out, but to listen to the people You have placed in my life to guide me.

Day 4 - Take Your Time

After a year of pampering, Esther was ready to go to the King.

"The king loved Esther more than all the women, and she won grace and favor in his sight more than all the virgins, so that he set the royal crown on her head and made her queen instead of Vashti. Then the king gave a great feast for all his officials and servants; it was Esther's feast. He also granted a remission of taxes to the provinces and gave gifts with royal generosity" (Esther 2:17-18).

He loved her so much he threw her a party, made a holiday in her name, and everyone walked away with a brand new car. He was into her. Those twelve months in the spa must have paid off! Can you imagine a year of prepping for something? It must have been similar to our senior year of high school when we were getting ready to go to college. Imagine a year of bulking up and working out in preparation for a recruiter to your chosen Big Ten school.

There are times where we are in waiting, but waiting is not passive. In high school, I made bad decisions about guys. In college it got worse, but then I decided to follow Jesus. For ten years I was free to live. I traveled all over the world on mission, wrote a book, and invested in young people. This time of waiting changed me, and it changed what I wanted in a partner.

What are the things that you want to hurry? What areas of your life do you need to wait -- but not passively wait -- on?

Affirmation: God works in us as we patiently wait on him. It's worth it.
Prayer: God, help me to know that waiting develops character.

Day 5 - Selling Out

Esther finds herself caught in the tug of war that most ethnic minorities find themselves in. We are taught to believe that in order to succeed we have to hide or suppress our identity, learn to speak "right," and learn to dress "right." The alternative is to accept the consequences with being "cultural." Remember Esther was told to hide her identity. Now, years later, she has assimilated and has achieved status. That must have been some makeover.

Maybe when she arrived, people made fun of her. The harem girls may have been hard on her, telling her to comb her hair, or accusing her of being fresh off the boat. She was not Persian enough for the Persians; maybe she was too ethnic? But years later she was the queen of a powerful empire. From the ghetto to Wall Street! Maybe she changed her look, her way of speaking, and her language. Esther never goes back to her 'hood, but can you imagine if she did? Would the Jews accuse her of thinking that she was too good? Maybe she would be accused of not being Jewish enough for the Jews, not ethnic enough. I know many of the youth in our urban community are made to feel like "other" if they have achieved academically or in an extra-curricular way. This is absurd. As if a person of color is not compatible with becoming an intelligent and driven scholar. Youth today must work hard not to internalize negative stereotypes that their peers have been duped by.

What about you? All of us have had to navigate two cultures in some capacity. It may be racial, socio-economic, or related to our faith. Have you ever been accused of being a sell out? Have you accused someone of selling out? What is behind the discomfort, and how can your faith inform you?

Affirmation: I must never allow other people to tell me who I am; only God can do that.
Prayer: Lord, search my heart and help me to deeply know where I am feeling excluded or making others feel excluded. Heal me.

Day 6 - Understanding Prejudice

Prejudice begins with anger, fear, and mistrust of a person, but then it extends onto the whole group. We embrace stereotypes that turn people into the "other" and dehumanize them based off of the color of their skin, their language, their immigration status, their customs, or any other difference. Instead of accepting the beauty of diversity, we alienate one another. Haman, the king's official in our story, tried to get rid of the Jews. What were his reasons for wanting to destroy them? Haman, filled with hate, wanted to annihilate a whole race because he felt threatened by their presence. It's stupid given that they were a community with no power and were already marginalized by society. Haman went to the king and told him that there was a group of people that had different laws and customs, which were a threat to him; and the king gave him permission to take care of it. Haman was excited about the results because the empire at that time was so big that virtually the whole race would have been wiped out.

We may not necessarily pursue physical harm to those who are different from us, but we do contribute to prejudice and mistrust across differences, when we allow ourselves to participate in things that offend the person God has made. Reflect on your own perspectives of certain groups, and confess ways you have contributed to "isms" -- racism, sexism, and classism.

Affirmation: As God's people, we are called to be people of reconciliation and unity.
Prayer: Lord, give me the grace I need to stand up for others when I hear people speak or act poorly against them.

Day 7 - Don't Take It into Your Own Hands

It may seem trivial that Haman wanted to axe an entire race because one Jew, Mordecai, would not bow down to him and show him honor. Or is it? Actually, it was a big deal because Haman was disrespected in public. Persian culture is an honor-based culture, which means that one's honor is all you had. Haman had to make sure that the punishment was severe in order to show that he was someone who deserved to be respected. Haman was trying to show how cruel he could be by persecuting the Jews during Passover. Jews retained their cultural identity over the course of time through their feasts and celebrations. Those celebrations were especially invaluable when the people no longer had a land to live in or a temple in which to worship. Just as the Jews were celebrating deliverance from their great enemies of the past, the Egyptians, they were hearing about the destruction to come. Haman was trying to break them. Haman reminds me of some youth in my community. Respect is all they have, and they go to great lengths to maintain it. If for example, someone strikes them, they strike back. If they don't, they will be seen as weak, and so they retaliate out of fear and honor.

In what circumstances do we do this?

Affirmation: God has got my back; leaning on him is not weak!
Prayer: Help me to trust You God, that You will avenge me, and that You are my rock and refuge in times of trouble.

Day 8 - Cover It Up -- Cover up the Mess

When Mordecai learned that the Jews would be destroyed, he "tore his clothes and put on sackcloth and ashes, and went out into the midst of the city, and he cried out with a loud and bitter cry. He went up to the entrance of the king's gate, for no one was allowed to enter the king's gate clothed in sackcloth" Esther 4:1-2. By making a scene, he wanted to ensure that his protest was noticed by the Persians. His spectacle embarrassed Esther and made her extremely ashamed. She sent her servant to tell Mordecai to get dressed and pull himself together. She even sent him some nice Persian brand clothes. It's not clear if she knew why he was upset. What was going on in Esther's head? What was she ashamed of? Was she afraid for Mordecai? Did she care at all? Did she feel bad for him or want to comfort him? After so long in the palace, had she forgotten who she was? Think of the last time you were embarrassed by someone's expression of faith or outrage at injustice. Maybe you saw someone on the street preaching, or you overheard someone on the bus witnessing. I know it is appropriate to be ashamed of the downfalls of the church, but I'm talking about just Christian stuff that embarrasses us. Do we ask people who are standing up and making bold moves for their faith to cover it up? In our story, what was Esther ashamed of?

Affirmation: We can't ask people to hide their beliefs or perspectives even when we are put out.
Prayer: Dear God, thank you for the community of witnesses that confronts me with my shame and invites me to boldness.

Day 9 - Not My People

When the crisis hits Esther's people, five years have already had passed. Imagine what life is like for the Jewish orphan girl who ends up in the palace where she was protected, and had found favor with people. Life is cushy in the palace! Or was Esther just surviving within her palace prison where she was not free to be anything but what they expected. Esther was fourth generation Jewish–Persian. For 120 years, her community had resided in a foreign land to which they had been forced to adapt. Though deeply assimilated to Persian culture, Esther was still a Jew. And now, she had been away from her community and part of an elite lifestyle that did not resemble the neighborhood from which she came. Esther felt displacement at many levels. Displacement will mess with you.

When I was getting my degree, there were no other Latino students in my program and only a handful in the entire institution. One morning when I got to campus early, I realized that the only people who came from my neighborhood arrived at 5:00 a.m. to clean the floors and empty the garbage cans. This made me wonder who my people really were. Were they my fellow students or my neighbors? I interacted with both groups, but felt caught in between. Like Esther, I belong to a displaced, marginalized group of exiles (immigrants) in a foreign land, unprotected and disliked. I know what it is like to have questions about my people both racially and spiritually. I did not grow up in the church, so there was and still is a lot about church culture that I just don't get. I often feel more comfortable with un-churched people than "churchy" people. Did I mention that I'm a pastor? Maybe you too feel caught between two communities trying to wrestle with who your people are. Maybe you feel displaced at church, school, or on your neighborhood block.

Affirmation: Belonging is an important part of our identity journey.
Prayer: Thank you for giving me experiences to help me reflect on who my people are.

Day 10 - Knock Offs

Did your mom ever make you buy a pair of sneakers at Payless? It was so embarrassing, when all of your friends were wearing Nike and Vans and you were forced to wear knock-offs. The idea of a good knock-off, whether it's a purse or cologne, is that the brand look-alike can "fool" people into believing it is the real thing. I survived junior high and high school without ever owning brand name jeans, purses or shoes. My parents were not willing to rack up credit card debt so that I could "fool" people into believing I had the money that others had. We lived in such an affluent context that I would never have been able to compete anyway. While we lived a modest lifestyle, we also occasionally had a season with government cheese. As if being different racially was not enough, I was "poor" in the suburbs. I regularly got mad at my parents for not giving me an item, a trip, or a car. I was ruthless in complaining about what my friends had that I did not have.

Now that I have resources, I have no interest in brands and overspending for the purpose of impressing others. I am free to live simply and invest my finances in programs that provide jobs for youth, housing for families, and a gospel witness in my urban neighborhood. My life experiences shaped me deeply. I went from being ashamed of my socio-economic upbringing to being thankful.

Esther clearly moved up in the world financially. She went from the Jewish ghetto lifestyle to being the most powerful woman in a kingdom that included many countries. I am sure that her modest upbringing affected the way she viewed a life of power and privilege.

Have you ever been mad or ashamed at your family's financial status? Have you thought about how God is using your experiences to shape your character?

Affirmation: I will not be ashamed of my upbringing; I will ask how it might be a benefit.
Prayer: Thank You, God, for promising to use everything in my life for Your glory and my good.

Day 11 - Code-Switching

Code switching is the practice of moving back and forth between two languages or dialects. Growing up we spoke "Spanglish" at home, which meant that our conversations would fluidly move back and forth from Spanish to English, and we didn't even notice it was happening unless we had friends over who didn't understand what we were saying. We were happy speaking, as well as listening to music or news, in both languages. Code switching, which explains how dialogue spans culture, allows us to get along with or fit in with people in different places. Esther would have been a master at code switching. She had grown up in a Jewish neighborhood and was raised by her cousin who clearly had a deep connection to his faith and heritage. Esther was tutored for a year under Hegai, who was in charge of the harem. Esther had been queen for about four years and hosted many gatherings for powerful Persian people. As queen she would have had to walk and talk the part. My guess is that when she spoke to Mordecai, she did not talk the way she did when she was around powerful people in the palace. It's kind of like she had to talk one way at work, and was able to talk in a way that was more comfortable and relaxed at home, because at home people knew the real Esther. This did not make Esther a hypocrite; it made her wise. Her skills in code switching allowed her to freely flow between audiences in order to get her job done.

Have you had the experience of code switching in culture and language? How do you do this in your witness of God? Are you able to speak about Him to un-churched people in ways that make sense, or is your language so religious that people can't understand what you are saying? How can you learn to adapt your language so that the gospel message is heard?

Affirmation: Learning to speak different languages and navigate between cultures are skills that are effective in gospel witness.

Prayer: God, give me wisdom and tutors that will help me to communicate in ways that help Your word to be heard.

Day 12 - Don't Tell Anyone

On her way out the door to the beauty contest, Esther was told by her father (cousin) not to reveal her identity. What confusing advice to take in from a parent who is supposed to love everything about you. Why would he ask her to hide who she was? Should she be ashamed of her race, ethnicity, or social status?

When I read that scene in the story it automatically brought me to my first day of grade school when my mom said to me, on my way out the door, "Sandrita, don't tell anyone you're Latino because you can pass." My mother was afraid for me because she knew how cruel the world was. She knew that the world judges us based on where we live, how we look, who our parents are, the color of our skin, the language that we speak, how "well" we speak, our educational status or citizenship, and if we have been in trouble with the law. She knew that telling people where I came from would potentially cause me to be rejected and discriminated against, and she wanted me to be accepted. Isn't that what every parent wants for their kid?

Mordecai also wanted to give Esther the best shot at being accepted; that is why he told her to hide her true identity. He had a strong ethnic and religious identity, and was not ashamed of being Jewish or standing up for his beliefs. That is why he wasn't willing to bow to Haman. He was, however, a realist and knew that Esther's identity would have stood in her way of becoming queen. If he could just get Esther in the door of the palace, she could later decide to reveal more. She didn't need to over share from the get go. Mordecai had street smarts!

Affirmation: Listening to wise advice does not mean I am selling out.
Prayer: Dear God, I want to accept all aspects of who You've made me, and learn to be smart when I reveal parts of who I am.

Day 13 - Unwelcomed Intruders

Our society has a way of treating people who are unwelcomed. Whether they are immigrants, ex-offenders, or just socially awkward people in our schools, we make people feel like the "other." When my family moved from a diverse urban setting to a predominantly white suburb, it was clear we did not fit in. The pain that I experienced as a child when people called me "spick" or "drug-dealer" was worse than when they destroyed our lawn or stole my bike. It wasn't just the children either; the parents made sure we knew we were less than them by the way they spoke to us. These traumatic experiences were buried deep inside until recently at a conference someone used the word "unwelcomed intruders" while speaking of the "browning of the suburbs." I immediately began to weep. I knew well what it meant to feel that way.

Esther belonged to a people who were second-class citizens. They had been taken over, exiled, and mistreated. The good news is that God has always taken care of the people on the outside. In this story, God protected them and saved them from death through Esther. Imagine the pain Esther felt when she thought back on the experiences of her people and their oppression. What might it be like to constantly feel unwelcomed? In what ways or spaces have you felt unwelcomed? What have you participated in that has made others feel like the "other"? How should knowing that God is on the side of those who are cast aside change us?

Affirmation: God is present with those who are marginalized by others.
Prayer: God, thank You for being on the side of the oppressed, help me to join You.

Day 14 - Where Is God?

God is not mentioned anywhere in the book of Esther. He doesn't come in a cloud or in fire or even with a gentle wind. He is not a character, but a director of this film. For the Jews, whose history included many tragic incidents, the book became a source of hope, and the events it records are celebrated annually in the festival of Purim. It is read even today to commemorate God's work in delivering His people. When Haman's name is mentioned in the Purim liturgy, congregations respond with loud banging, shouting, and stamping of feet. "Boo Haman!" Not surprisingly, Jews know the story of Esther better than other parts of the Old Testament.

When I was in college, my boyfriend of six years broke up with me. We had an extremely unhealthy relationship, but I just could not break it off. My faith was weak, and I felt spiritually "dry." That made sense given the fact that I was not honoring God with my decisions in that relationship. Where was God? He was right there! Despite the fact that I did not have the courage, God worked it out for me to be free from that relationship. It hurt, but it set me free to pursue my dreams.

We, too, may go through periods of our lives where we feel God is not present. We may feel his absence, but his work happens through community, through mentors, and through our decisions to be faithful to his mission. You may feel like you need deliverance for your community from forces that are oppressing you. You may just feel alone or frustrated with God's silence.

Affirmation: God is at work in saving and restoring his people even when we experience his absence.
Prayer: Where are You God? Help me to believe you are present with me and for me.

Day 15 - Know Your Champions

Esther had some champions that had her back. Hegai coached her in what to do and say, helping her to become desirable to the king. Esther likely also had servants, like the one who was sent to give a message to Mordecai. They kept the secrets that would reveal her identity. Then there was Moredcai, who was her ultimate champion. We all need people who support and motivate us. My friend, Kristi, had an eighth grade school counselor as her champion. She attended a diverse school, which was made up of forty percent white, forty percent Latino and about twenty percent black students. One day the school counselor unexpectedly called an assembly with only the black students. Being African American himself, he wanted to have a talk with them about what it meant to go beyond what they've always been told--that they were not smart enough, that they were too ghetto, and that they were too poor. The counselor later called each of them individually into his office. He encouraged my friend Kristi on her track record and told her how successful she could be. Kristi just needed to believe in herself and not to listen to what others said. He also told her that she would make history through her achievements in the community, which came to pass even before she left high school. This type of encouragement helped Kristi believe in a greater call. Kristi's counselor back when she was in eighth grade was an effective champion.

Who's got your back? Who is cheering for you and believing better things for you?

Affirmation: Champions encourage us and advocate for us in the journey.
Prayer: God, thank You for always sending the right person to help me along the way.

Day 16 - A Hard Word

Mordecai instructed Esther to go into the king's presence to beg for mercy and plead with him for her people. When she refused, Mordecai pointed out that she was in a position to solve the problem, and even if it was costly she had to do it. He said, "Do not think that because you are in the king's house you alone of all the Jews will escape. For if you remain silent at this time, relief and deliverance for the Jews will arise from another place, but you and your father's family will perish" (Esther 4:13-14). Mordecai had to tell Esther the truth.

That's what parents and mentors do. It's never easy or fun, but sometimes love comes in the form of a hard word. I have an insightful and winsome woman who mentors me. When we are in public venues together I watch her interactions to learn how she handles critical situations and people. One time when we were attending a speaker's dinner at a conference, she taught me something I'll never forget. After the evening of networking and connection with other leaders in our field, she took me aside to debrief the time we had. My mentor affirmed me and encouraged my ability to connect with others.

Then she did something impactful. She grabbed the shoulder of my jacket and said, "This coat has got to go. This says 'college student.' You are leader in the community and need to get a coat that reflects that." She was looking out for my reputation and image. That was not the first or last time a hard word was given alongside encouragement.

When was the last time someone gave you a hard word that left your jaw hanging open? Do you have the stomach to allow hard words to influence you?

Affirmation: Truth is often hard to hear, but it is necessary for molding us into our call.
Prayer: Dear God, give me a humble heart that is open to critique and the resolve to change where needed.

Day 17 - Real Friends (Not the Online Kind)

Esther finally did agree to approach the king to plea on behalf of her people, but she had to get a plan together first. Notice that the first thing she did was to ask for the involvement of her faith community. She said, "Go, gather together all the Jews who are in Susa, and fast for me. Do not eat or drink for three days, night or day. My attendants and I will fast as you do. When this is done, I will go to the king, even though it is against the law. And if I perish, I perish" Esther 4:16. Esther started with calling her community into the struggle with her. Esther involved her whole community because she knew how important it was to have support and prayers.

Members of small groups that we belong to are serious about supporting one another. We have provided housing for one another, prayed for jobs, celebrated weddings, grieved the loss of a baby, and gathered for prayer late at night when one was in need. Do you have a small group you can go to for support? Considering the many decisions we have to make in life, a group of people we can talk to and have pray for us is very important.

Affirmation: I should not go at it on my own – I will connect to a community that strengthens me.
Prayer: Enable me, dear God, to be vulnerable enough to ask for help when I need it.

Day 18 - Sticking Your Neck Out

The phrase "sticking your neck out" came from the way chickens were put on the chopping block. It also describes a turtle risking his own safety when he sticks his neck out of the shell. Sticking your neck out is dangerous business. What's the most dangerous or risky thing you've ever been asked to do? Do you remember how afraid you were? Was it a life or death situation? In Esther's case, it was a death sentence. After she asks her community to fast and pray Esther said, "When this is done, I will go to the king, even though it is against the law. And if I perish, I perish" (Esther 4:16). She understood that the task that she had to complete to save her people would cost her life. That is a thrilling idea for someone else, not for us. We live through others' risks by watching movies where the hero risks his or her life on behalf of the moral good. The hero always seems to be good-looking and he or she gets it done with style; this is Esther.

What would it take for you to overcome your fear of what other people think so that you can start living a dangerous life of worship? What risks are God asking you to take in the next week? Year?

Affirmation: If we want to accomplish big things in life we have to take risks.
Prayer: Jesus, when I think about what You did for me on the Cross, I want to live a bolder faith.

Day 19 - Understanding Power

Power means many different things to different people. For some, power means success; for others, power is dangerous because it leads to corruption. There are many different kinds of control, including social, relational, political, and financial. There are two kinds of power we must understand how to navigate if we want to make a difference in the world. Legitimate power comes from a position of authority and can be exercised freely given the role people have. Influence, which is gained through relationships and reputation, is another form. Many of us would find life would be easier if we had more legitimate power, but a good leader can effectively create change with influence.

Think about Mordecai's understanding of power as he leads Esther to deliver her people. He knows that the legitimate power is in the hands of Haman and the king. What can Esther, a woman, really do? Yet, her cousin asks her to approach the king and ask him for a favor. Mordecai knew that Esther had influence; she pleased the king with her beauty and her character. Remember that Esther had a holiday in her honor. Mordecai knew that even though her status as queen was not worth much, her influence could be great. He also believed the God of Israel was on their side. Why is it important to understand systems of worldly power even as believers? How can we confront systems of power?

Affirmation: Each of us has some form of power we can use when God calls us to difficult situations.
Prayer: Praise God that He has all influence and authority over every system of power.

Day 20 - Imposter Syndrome

Sometimes we don't step up to the task God presents before us because we suffer from "imposter syndrome." The evidence shows that we are qualified, but we remain convinced that the success we have achieved is just luck or people believing we are more competent than we are. We're afraid someone will find out that we are frauds.

At a recent meeting of influential justice leaders, Pastor Fred confessed to me that he often felt intimidated by certain people with more education. Even coming to the meeting with all of these important influencers made him feel like an "imposter." When I heard that, I was sad; he was the most credible voice on the subject we were discussing and people valued his opinion. When Mordecai sent Esther the text, "Real life going on out here: you might want to look outside your window. We need help out here," she replies saying, "That's impossible." She is expressing doubt, "Who me? What do I have to say? What could I possibly do?" What situations make you feel like you will be discovered as an imposter? What keeps you from believing that you actually are qualified?

Affirmation: Feeling inadequate is normal; but I must try to discover what is causing it.
Prayer: God, help me to believe that You have given me everything I need for success.

Day 21 - Use What Your Daddy Gave You

Esther had to embrace how God created her and what God had given her. She was hot. She is described as "having a lovely figure and was beautiful." Her look pleased the king. Clearly she had nothing to do with how good-looking she was. She was born with the artistry of her creator. This was beyond her control. The other thing Esther had to embrace was her experience in the palace. Whether this was a pleasant experience or a prison, she had no choice. All the women were told to parade before the king. However, the diplomatic wisdom she gained would help her cause later on in the story. Even the insider view she had been given was beyond her control.

At some point in our lives we all have to acknowledge that our natural abilities and experiences are gifts from God. Then you can "use what your mama gave you." One of my brothers is an outgoing artist. He is creative and can draw the attention of a crowd with his presence. Another brother is a more reserved emergency room doctor. They are like two sides of a coin. Each one of them was given a different set of gifts, so naturally their calling in life has reflected their distinctiveness. One is utilizing art in therapy and coming alongside urban youth to help them tell their stories. The other has worked in one of our country's busiest emergency rooms, and his steady temperament allows him to stay calm when he is treating a patient with multiple gunshot wounds.

Romal says it this way, "God created you to be who you are and to live fully and unapologetically. Don't be ashamed of who you are because of what other people might think of you."

Affirmation: God was pleased to create me to be who I am uniquely.

Prayer: Thank You, God, for making me who I am. I accept all the gifts and experiences You have given to me.

Day 22 - "Frenemies" (Friends Who are Enemies)

Some people just make you mad. They don't let up, no matter what. Sometimes they're so hurtful or slanderous, causing you such frustration that you just want to write them out of your life. They may not even know they're doing it. In my life I've encountered many people who have wronged me, and I just wanted to get out of the relationship. Yet, due to job assignments or mutual friendships, I was stuck; but it's been hard to continue to do life and ministry in their presence. Imagine Esther, though, having to be social with someone who wanted her and her entire people killed. When Esther invites the king to the banquet she also invites Haman. What is she trying to do? Couldn't she just speak with the King privately? I'm sure she had a way to do it. Given Haman's recent promotion and connection with the King, Esther's invitation to Haman is strategic. She wants the king to be in the best mood for her announcement. And, if she didn't invite Haman, the king may not have granted her request to come to the banquet. Also, her invitation ensures Haman has no idea what's happening, as we can see from how he brags to his wife and friends. In addition, Esther probably knows scripture, which teaches that people who think they're hot stuff get knocked down by God. So inviting Haman only makes him fall more in love with himself, so in love that he has to brag about it to his wife and friends. God has a purpose for everyone, even his enemies. Our job is not to try to control the situation, but, as Esther did with fasting and prayer, get wisdom from God as to how to interact with those people in our lives. Who is your Haman? How might God be calling you to interact with him/her?

Affirmation: God gives wisdom and grace to deal with our enemies.
Prayer: God, help me to be wise and Christ-like with those who are hard to deal with.

Day 23 - For Such a Time as This

In the famous line from the book of Esther, Mordecai confronts her with this question, "And who knows but that you have come to your royal position for such a time as this" (4:14)? He has broken it down for her. First, her location in the palace will not protect her. Second, God is going to deliver his people no matter what. Esther hears that victory is not dependent on her. Someone else will get to be the hero in the story if she does not act. Her exact position and relationship to the king at this exact time in their history is the perfect combination. She acts. God is calling us to have courage. It is exciting to be the right person at the right place in the right time. We get to participate in the work of transforming places and rescuing people.

What about you? What is happening in your world that is an invitation to act? In which places is God asking you to be more courageous? Is he inviting you to speak out as a Christian voice in your school or workplace? Is he asking you to stand up for injustice somewhere?

Affirmation: When I accept God's call and act with courage, I will be able to accomplish great things.
Prayer: Thank You God for being the agent of victory, and thank You for inviting me to participate in the change.

Day 24 - Hustle or Woo

Esther's got game! Watching her work in chapters five and six is epic. She understands that anyone who "approaches the king in the inner court" can be put to death, so she doesn't "approach" him. Instead the passage says, "Esther put on her royal robes and 'stood' in the inner court of the palace, in front of the king's hall. The king was sitting on his royal throne in the hall, facing the entrance. When he saw Queen Esther standing in the court, he was pleased with her and held out to her the gold scepter that was in his hand. So Esther 'approached'" (5:1-2). Esther clearly had the ability to "woo," -- to win people over. She knew that getting in her fancy dress and being noticed by the king would win her an audience with the king. When he asks Esther what she wants, offering right away up to half of his kingdom, she merely requests his presence and invites him to a party. Once she's got his attention, she'll bring up her need. Now that is smart. Imagine how many times the king is hustled for money, land, and power. He is bombarded with favors all day long, but Esther just wants to treat him well. Instead of hustling him, she is winning him over naturally and shrewdly. I appreciate the difference between Haman's hustle of the king to get what he wanted, and Esther's winsome and prudent winning over. I hate getting hustled, don't you? You can tell when someone is manipulatively trying to get something from you; their very presence seems fake. How can you authentically win people over? Do you pay attention to others? Are you invested in what they like and don't like? Are you able to speak to them in ways that values their unique personality?

Affirmation: We need to be smart and think carefully about how we pursue our goals.
Prayer: Lord, help me to be as shrewd as snakes and as innocent as doves (Matthew 10).

Day 25 - Using All of You

Esther used everything her mama gave her to put a strategy into place. She utilized not only her beauty, but her political savvy and natural intellect as well. She had thrown parties for the king, even inviting her enemy Haman; she treated them well. And now the king really wanted to know how he could please her. Then Esther revealed the situation, "If I have found favor with you, your Majesty, and if it pleases you, grant me my life—this is my petition" (Esther 7:3). She then asks on behalf of her people as well, but I'm pretty sure the king could not hear anything after the first request. How could it be? His lovely and winsome queen was going to die? No, he would not have this. The last time he searched for a queen, it took him a year to find one, and he thought Esther was perfect. This is the climax of Esther's task -- the big reveal. The fact that she is a Jew becomes the foundation for salvation for her people.

God, in his sovereignty, has given you personal experiences that have made you who you are. They are gifts from God that enable you to glorify Him and work for His purposes. What foundation has God laid for you? What experiences, passion, and gifts has He given you? What opportunities do you have access to that no one else may have? How will you use those?

Affirmation: There is freedom in understanding and embracing our identity and living into it.
Prayer: Thank You for the hope that there is a plan for all of my experiences.

Day 26 - Mi Gente!

Esther's purpose was to help not only herself but also her people. After she pleas for herself she continues, "And spare my people—this is my request. For I and my people have been sold to be destroyed, killed, and annihilated" Esther 7:3-4. Esther understood that the true purpose in life is not about helping yourself, but also about helping the people in your community. As Romal says, "God wants the same thing for you that God wanted for Esther: to stop hiding who you are and to be courageous enough to stand up for the people who need you—your family, community, friends, and yourself. When you make the decision to be unapologetically yourself and to do the things that you know in your heart are right, that's what gives you inner peace and the ability to go out and do what God created you to do." This is seen in the courageous work that young undocumented people are doing on behalf of their community. They are using their journeys of pain and lack of security to mobilize the church toward immigration reform. They are not just advocating on their own behalf, but on the behalf of others in their community.

Affirmation: We belong to a community (ethnic, faith, etc.) that deserves our commitment.
Prayer: Help me Lord to see beyond my own welfare to the well-being of my people.

Day 27 - Find Your Place and Purpose

I often feel out of place or like I don't belong. Examples of this weave throughout my life, from being the only woman on a preaching team; recognizing that I'm the only Latino in my seminary class; hearing everyone around me use big, fancy words that I later have to look up in a dictionary; seeing all my high school friends with fancy clothes and first class vacations while I'm stuck at home shopping at Family Dollar. But what I've found as God has led me to ministry around the world is that there is something only I could do. In 2012, I was invited to Swaziland, Africa to help film a video about the work God was doing amongst the poor. Some people would be very uncomfortable, not having many experiences overseas or amongst truly poor people. However, much of my family is overseas, so I was able to engage people and make the connections necessary for the project. It was something only I could do. I even got a live chicken out of it as a gift -- really – ask me some time.

We see from Ether's story that God was arranging situations in her young life so she could do amazing things for God and His people. The combination of her ethnic identity, her community, her access to the King, and the wisdom God gave her; God made her the perfect person for what God wanted to do. Think of your own life. Where have you seen God at work setting you up to do something for Him? What are the things God is calling you to do that only you can do? Maybe you're a certain guy's only friend and he needs to hear the gospel. Maybe no one else in your family is helping a certain girl out but you are available. What are three things that God wants you to do right now that no one else can do?

Affirmation: God has arranged the situations in my life for His purposes.
Prayer: Give me wisdom to see what Your unique will is for me.

Day 28 - Finding Voice

Esther was a young woman who did not allow her youth to discredit her from making a difference for her people. Young people in our society have always been at the forefront of change. Truth be told, young people have headed up almost every major societal change across the globe. Young people need opportunities to find their voice and passions. A group of urban young people raised more than $20,000 to advocate for an end to police brutality. The group called "We Charge Genocide" was able to send eight members to the United Nations meeting to present on the experiences of youth of color. The Chicago-based activists came together to raise awareness against police brutality and stayed committed to their cause. Much like the "dreamers" in the fight for immigration reform, they used their voices to speak on behalf of the well-being of their community. How does voice get shaped? I know students in a local school are assigned a senior project to that focuses on a social topic of interest. The students in the school whom I have coached have worked on gender discrimination in the workplace, salary as well as racial discrimination, and mass incarceration. I would not be surprised if they remain advocates for those causes.

Affirmation: I won't let anyone look down on me because I am young, but instead, I will set an example for the believers in speech, in conduct, in love, in faith and in purity (1 Tim. 4:12).
Prayer: God, give me the courage to give voice to my passions no matter the cost.

Day 29 - Dealing with the Pain (Entry from God's Graffiti)

Esther had a lot of past pain to process. We don't get a deep glimpse into her personal pain through the story, but we know it is there. She was orphaned and that alone is pain that would have needed healing. As Romal says in *God's Graffiti,* "All of us are the products of our pasts. Pain cannot be completely avoided. But whether that pain includes the absence of our parents or the consequences of our own behaviors, we don't have to be prisoners of personal pain." What aspects of Esther's painful story can you identify with? We are all going to experience some measure of pain many times in our lives. So, how do we manage it? How do you learn from pain so that you are able to fulfill God's purpose for your lives? Be honest about your feelings. Accept the reality that you are sad and hurt and lonely. Get someone in your corner. Talk to someone who can understand your deepest and most personal thoughts and feelings. Talk to God. Ask God for strength to manage and overcome your pain. Connect your past and present pain. Understand how pain from your past will affect your behavior unless it is resolved. What pain is unresolved?

Affirmation: Pain cannot be avoided, but healing can be found.
Prayer: Jesus, You are the healer; help me to trust I can be honest with my pain.

Day 30 - Vision for Greatness

People who accept God's call and act with courage are able to accomplish great things. God saved a kingdom through an orphan. The story ends with King Xerxes avenging Esther, Mordecai, and their people. Esther was given Haman's estate; she rose from a poor marginalized orphan girl to the position of queen and owner, which women were not allowed to be. Mordecai went from death row to having his accuser executed on his chopping block. Mordecai also inherited his authority and job status at the right hand of the king; he went from outside the gate, to inside the inner court. And the Jews went from death to victory. Esther's actions also fueled a revival, given the power they saw exercised by the Jews. The passage in Esther 8: 15-17 says, "The city of Susa held a joyous celebration. For the Jews it was a time of happiness and joy, gladness and honor. In every province and in every city to which the edict of the king came, there was joy and gladness among the Jews, with feasting and celebrating. And many people of other nationalities became Jews because fear of the Jews had seized them." God worked it out for their good as he promises us. In the end, a holiday of remembrance was established for fasting and lament, as well as for the celebration of God's work; called the festival of Purim, it also honors the work of Esther and Mordecai. Jews have been able to hope in what can be, given their history and their heroism of faith. Esther's faithfulness and courage, despite her self-doubt and fear, has given hope to generations.

Affirmation: Every generation needs "Esthers" to lead them in lament and hope.
Prayer: Thank You for being a God who avenges wrong and works for good.

CHAPTER SEVEN

- JOSEPH -

SHAWN CASSELBERRY

Day 1 - Comparison is the Thief of Joy

Why do we think the grass is always greener on the other side? We spend a lot of energy trying to keep up with what's in style. What's hot? What's not? We want to keep abreast of some standard of what the good life is. But who decides that standard? Why do we try to keep up with "the Jones'?" Why do we compare ourselves to the measure of others? We need to realize the grass may seem greener on the other side, but everyone's grass is hiding bugs and dirt underneath the surface. Romans 12:1 says, "Do not be conformed to the patterns of this world, but be transformed by the renewing of your mind." When we live our lives by God's standard, we don't have to worry about living up to everyone else's guidelines. We don't have to fear we're missing out. Once you realize "cool" is manufactured by companies to convince you to buy their products, you realize you don't need all that stuff to be cool. You are loved as you are. You don't need to be prettier, more fashionable, or trendier than you already are. Once you live by God's standards, you are free from all other false criterions.

Affirmation: I am cool just as I am.
Prayer: Dear God, help me know I am loved as I am so I can be free from trying to be like everybody else.

Day 2 - Hurt

Johnny Cash remade a Nine Inch Nails song entitled "Hurt." The opening line is, "I hurt myself today, just to see if I still feel." It is easy to grow numb to the pain of the past. Sometimes we would rather not feel at all than to feel the pain. Sometimes we hurt ourselves just so we can feel something. We all have different ways we numb our pain. Instead of facing the pain, we end up stuffing our emotions down, ignoring them, hurting ourselves, or lashing out at others. Joseph had deep hurts. He was hated by his brothers and rejected by his family, and falsely accused of a crime he didn't commit. Maybe you have suffering. No matter how careful we go through life we will inevitably hurt and be hurt. We can let pain turn to anger and numbness

115

or we can start to give voice to our aching. Journaling is a great way to give voice to our pain. Expressing our anguish allows us to heal. Can you remember a time you hurt someone? Did you apologize? Did they forgive you? Has someone hurt you? How did you respond? Did you respond in the way you wish others responded to you? There's a lot of distress and sadness in the world. As they say, "hurt people, hurt people." We can end the cycle by facing our pain, expressing it, and choosing to walk toward forgiveness.

Affirmation: I am breaking the cycle by dealing with my pain.
Prayer: Lord, help me experience healing for my hurt by facing my pain and moving toward forgiveness.

Day 3 - God Is a Dreamer

God is a dreamer. We were created in the image of God so we are dreamers too. Because God is a dreamer, God likes speaking to us through dreams. We may not receive dreams exactly like Joseph did, but we all dream. We all have imagination. We all have hopes. I think God speaks to us through our dreams and desires. Proverbs 37:4 says, "Delight yourself in the Lord, and God will give you the desires of your heart." When we are in tune with God, then our desires and dreams become shaped by God. Have you ever noticed your desires or dreams changing? Do you recognize that what you used to desire so badly no longer satisfies you? I think as we walk with God, the Holy Spirit changes our desires and re-shapes our dreams. This is why it is important to pay attention to our dreams. God may be speaking through them. I see this in the "I Have a Dream" speech of Martin Luther King Jr. Dr. King had a dream of a world where people were not judged by their skin color but by the content of their character. He dreamed people of all cultural backgrounds could live in peace together. Can you see how God might have been shaping Dr. King's dreams and desires? What is your dream? How might God be shaping your visions for the future?

Affirmation: I am a dreamer.
Prayer: God, give me a vision for the world the way You would want it to be.

Day 4 - From Dream to Reality

We see in the story of Joseph that God speaks to us through dreams, but notice this: sometimes it takes a long time for the dream to become a reality. When God gives us a vision, it does not mean it will happen overnight. The dream is a starting point. God gives us a vision of the world and of ourselves the way God would want it to be. It is a visualization of how things can be if we continue to trust and follow God. Dreams are not guaranteed to happen. Dreams can die. Dreams are like flowers in a garden. If we do not cultivate them, they will not grow. If you want to see your vision become reality, it will take time and effort. Here are a couple of steps to realize your dream:

1. Write down the vision. In Habakkuk 2:2, the Lord replied, "Write down the vision and make it plain." This helps you stay focused on the vision and communicate it to others.

2. Come up with short-term and long-term goals that will get you there. It's good to have small first steps we can take right away as well as longer-term action steps.

3. Don't give up—most people quit when it gets hard. You will face adversity like Joseph did, but you have to persevere.

4. Ask God to guide, direct, strengthen, and support you. Don't ask God to just bless your idea, but seek God's wisdom and guidance throughout the process.

5. Learn from the failures. You will have setbacks and you will make mistakes. Learn from them.

6. See it through to the end, no matter how long it takes.

Affirmation: I can make my dream a reality.
Prayer: Lord, direct me as I pursue the vision You have placed in my heart.

Day 5 - Daddy's Boy

Were you closer to one of your parents? Were you a momma's boy or a daddy's girl? Joseph was a daddy's boy. Joseph's father favored him over his brothers, and Joseph knew it and Joseph's brothers knew it, too, and they hated him for it. It is okay for a son or daughter to feel closer to one parent over the other, but a parent should not favor one child over another child. When a parent showers more love on one child then it can create competition between the kids causing hurt, rejection, and pain. Parents are supposed to reflect God's love to us. They are supposed to love all their children like God does. The Bible says, "God does not show favoritism"

Romans 2:11, Acts 10:34. God does not love anyone more than another. God loves us all equally so we are all God's favorite. Although we make mistakes and choose to run from God, God is always inviting us back into a loving embrace. We are all God's daddy's boy or girl!

Affirmation: I am God's favorite.
Prayer: Lord, let your love sink into the deepest places of my heart.

Day 6 - Sibling Rivalry

Do you have a sibling or were you an only child? If you had brothers or sisters, did you ever experience sibling rivalry? This is when siblings compete against each other. They might fight for mom's or dad's attention and they may physically fight each other. I have an older sister and we definitely had sibling rivalry. We would have epic physical battles. We would throw things, slam doors, tell on each other, and wrestle like we were in the WWE (World Wrestling Entertainment, Inc.). Eventually, I grew taller and stronger and my sister realized it was smarter to be friends than enemies. Instead of shutting her door and shutting me out of her life like she used to, she started opening up. In high school, we started talking more and becoming better friends, realizing that we were on the same team. When we stopped fighting, we were actually able to get to know each other. Now, we are really close friends even though we live many states away. When Cain killed his brother Abel in the book of Genesis, he asked God, "Am I my brother's keeper?" He wanted to pretend he was not responsible for looking after his brother. How do you treat your brothers or sisters? If you're older, are you a good role model for your younger siblings? How do you want your relationship to be? If you are an only child, do you have any friends who are like a brother or sister to you? If you have a sibling rivalry, maybe it's time to call a ceasefire and end the war. Wouldn't you rather be friends than enemies?

Affirmation: I am my brother's keeper.
Prayer: Lord, help me to love my brothers and sisters so we can develop a true friendship.

Day 7 - Letting Go of Ego

There's a difference between believing in yourself and believing you are better than everyone else. Having pride in yourself, your work, or your accomplishments is good. But pride can be destructive when we start believing our own hype and thinking we are better than everyone else. Oftentimes we go back and forth between thinking too highly or too lowly of ourselves. We either suffer from an inferiority complex (deflated ego) or a superiority complex (inflated ego). It's okay to think we're good at something, but that does not mean we are better than other people. Everyone has equal value so no one has greater worth than another. If we are not careful, our pride can come across as arrogance. Joseph had a positive self-image that bordered on a superiority complex. When Joseph shared his dream of ruling over his brothers, it naturally made his brothers angry. We have to keep our ego in check, whether we are playing a pickup game of basketball or running a business. James 4:6 says, "God opposes the proud but gives grace to the humble." Being humble does not mean we think lesser of ourselves than others, but that we see ourselves as equal with everyone else. This requires us to let go of our egos. When we let our egos go then we can appreciate the value of every person.

Affirmation: I am not better or worse than anyone.
Prayer: Lord, help me not think too highly or too lowly of myself.

Day 8 - Growing into Our Dreams

What's your dream job? What would you do even if you didn't get paid for it? What is it that you can't stop doing? For some it might be singing, participating in sports, counseling, teaching, or investing money. For me, it's writing. Though I never thought of myself as a writer, I was good at creative writing in middle school because I had a wild imagination. And, I've kept a journal for the last twenty years, but only recently did I realize it was because I couldn't *stop* writing. Eventually, the passion and purpose God plants inside of us have to come out. Joseph had a gift for dreams and leadership. He couldn't *stop* dreaming. He couldn't *stop* leading. Our dreams help us know who we are; our dreams are signs from God as to how we've been made. This means, when we follow our dreams we just might be following God. That doesn't mean the journey is a clear path. Joseph had the dream but it took a lot of pain and heartache to fulfill it. A dream is not fulfilled overnight. It takes practice, planning, and patience. It takes time. Don't give up on your dream. Let it develop and grow. Like Joseph, sometimes we have to grow into our dreams.

Affirmation: I have gifts just waiting to be discovered.
Prayer: Dear God, give me patience to follow my dream even when it takes time.

Day 9 - Dream or Nightmare

How do we tell a good dream from a bad dream? What if our dream is really a nightmare? When I was in middle school my dream was to be rich; filthy rich to be exact. I wanted to make money. I drew a picture of my dream home: It had a pool shaped like a dollar sign, a six-car garage with Lamborghinis, amusement parks, and everything else I could possibly want or imagine. I was so into money that I signed my name: $hawn (this was many years before Kei$ha)! But eventually God gave me another dream. It was a dream for how my life could be lived following my passion to serve people, fight for justice, and use my voice and writing to speak out on behalf of others. This dream has led me to a fruitful life. I've travelled to cities and countries across the world and met amazing people; I've seen how ministries are addressing poverty and injustice among the world's most vulnerable. I get to interact with young people who want to see their lives transformed by serving others. If I had followed my original dream, it would have turned into a nightmare. I would have been happy momentarily, but I would not have the same sense of meaning and purpose that I have now. We have to learn to tell the difference between good dreams and God dreams.

Affirmation: My life has meaning and purpose.
Prayer: Lord, help me not only to discern between good and bad dreams, but between good and God dreams.

Day 10 - Good for ~~Nothing~~ Something

Have you ever been told you are no good? Have you ever been told you'll never amount to anything? People have the power to speak blessings or curses over our lives. Words are very powerful. There was an experiment conducted to see if words had the power to make someone better at basketball. The coach started telling the worst player on the team that he was the best player on the team and his teammates played along, also telling the player he was really good at basketball. By the end of the season, the worst player had become the star of the team. The power of words influenced how he played. When we realize God speaks blessings over our lives, it has the power to change us. In Jeremiah 29:11, God says, "For I know the plans I have for you, plans to prosper you and not to harm you, plans to give you a future and hope." God has plans for you. God wants to give you a future and a hope. This knowledge has the potential to change the way you live your life. Even if no one else speaks positive words over our lives, we have God. Once we start listening to God's words we can speak these words over our own lives: "God has a plan for my life. God wants to prosper me. God wants to give me a future." We spend a lot of time tearing ourselves down, but instead we should speak positive things into our lives. There's enough negativity outside us that we don't need the negativity inside us. If you believe in yourself, people will start to believe in you, too. But even if they don't, know that God says you are good, and you are made for something great.

Affirmation: God has a good future in store for me.
Prayer: Instead of dwelling on negative words, help me to focus on positive words.

Day 11 - Fight of Your Life

Rocky is the ultimate boxing movie. If you've seen the Rocky movies, you know there's a similar storyline through each movie. Rocky faces a challenger who he has to fight. Most of the time, the challenger appears to be stronger or he seems to have the edge on Rocky. Rocky has to overcome his fear, go through intense training, and face the opponent. During the fight, Rocky always gets knocked down, but he never stays down; he gets back up and ends the match victorious. You can count on it. It's why we love to see these kinds of movies. Our lives often play out in the same way. We are constantly challenged and taunted by giants who look bigger than us. We can back down, or we can face our fears and train so we can become better. Leaders are learners. The word "disciple" means to be a learner. To be a Christian is to be a learner. We have to trust that the training and practice is putting us in the best position to be successful. Keep your focus, keep working at it, and then be prepared. But know that you will have a moment where you will be knocked down and you will have the wind taken from your sails. Maybe you get an "F" on a test or you don't get selected for the basketball team. Maybe you get rejected at your first choice for college. You have to decide if you will stay down or fight like Rocky and Joseph. Joseph was down, but he didn't stay down. To see your dream come to life, you have to fight for it.

Affirmation: I am a fighter.
Prayer: Lord, when I'm knocked down, help me to not stay down but instead to get up and keep working hard at my dream.

Day 12 - Sold Out

Has anyone ever sold you out? Chances are we haven't experienced anything like Joseph. Probably few of us were almost killed by our brothers and sold into slavery. But, we've probably been betrayed. We've been led to believe one thing and realized we've been lied to. Cheated. Sold out. Jesus got sold out by one of his closest friends for thirty pieces of silver. There's no guarantee that we won't also feel the sting of betrayal. You might have a friend lie to you or a girlfriend or boyfriend cheat on you. Maybe your friend will cheat on you with your girlfriend or boyfriend. Betrayal can cause us to shut down and shut off our emotions. We can refuse to love or trust again. We can close ourselves off from others and live in our own protected world. Joseph kept his heart open. He did not let the betrayal shut him down. He kept his focus on making good choices and pursuing the path God set out for him. He chose to forgive his brothers rather than let his anger and hatred fester. Being betrayed hurts. It's not easy to get over and it takes time. Have you been betrayed? Are you still holding onto bitterness or anger?

Affirmation: I will keep my heart open.
Prayer: Lord, take away my bitterness so I can pursue the path You have for me.

Day 13 - Becoming Whole

Why did Jesus heal people? Why did Jesus give sight to the blind? Heal lepers? Why did Jesus spend so much time addressing people's physical needs? Why didn't Jesus just come and preach sermons or give them steps to get to Heaven? Because God doesn't just want us to believe all the right things, He wants to see our whole lives transformed. Healing is part of the nature of God. God is wholeness and we cannot be around God without experiencing healing. Jesus does not let us to continue on our faith journey without addressing our hurt and seeing us become whole. None of us chose where we were born. The blind man Jesus heals in John 9 didn't do anything to be blind, though Jesus' disciples assumed he was blind because he or his family had sinned. But that is not why he was blind. Jesus stands up for the blind man and says, "Neither this man or his family sinned, but this happened so that the works of God might be displayed" John 9:3. We start where we are regardless of our choice. But despite the setbacks in our life, God is able to do mighty works in our lives. God desires for all of us to move from brokenness to wholeness. The past can't be changed but we can write a new script for the future. Healing comes when we let God work in us, especially in the deep places of pain. God won't force healing on us. We have to choose it for ourselves. We have to open our hearts for God to come in and heal us.

Affirmation: God wants me to be whole.
Prayer: Lord, make me whole.

Day 14 - Never Look Back

Did you ever threaten to run away from home? Did you ever think, "I'm going to run away and never come back?" Did you ever actually try running away from home? Sometimes we can't leave physically so we check out mentally. We all have different ways of dealing with tough situations and hard family lives, as we create different coping mechanisms to deal with the pain. Being sarcastic and cynical is one way we might navigate an undesirable situation. We might act like we don't care or that we're tough enough to handle it to keep ourselves from getting hurt. In his book *God's Graffiti,* Romal wanted to leave home and never look back. He wanted to forget the places of pain, shame, and hurt. Joseph wanted to cut off his family because they had cut him off. He wanted to start a new life and never look back. But instead, Joseph faced his family and his feelings. He wept over the pain from the past and then extended forgiveness. This allowed for his family to be reconciled and to start a new chapter. In 2 Corinthians 5:18, it says, "For God has reconciled us to himself through Christ, and given us the ministry of reconciliation." God forgave us and wants us to forgive others. When we forgive others we become agents of reconciliation.

Affirmation: I am forgiven therefore I will forgive.
Prayer: Lord, help me become an agent of reconciliation in my relationships.

Day 15 - Falsely Accused

After Joseph was sold into slavery he started working for Potiphar. Joseph was hard working and responsible so Potiphar trusted him with watching over his house. While Joseph worked at Potiphar's house, Potiphar's wife would pressure him to have sex with her. When Joseph didn't sleep with her, she falsely accused him of trying to come on to her, which led to his arrest. If Joseph would have given in to Potiphar's wife's sexual advances, Joseph may have avoided prison; but instead, Joseph chose to do the right thing and ended up paying for it. Sometimes doing the right thing costs us. Saying no to the pressures of friends or boyfriends and girlfriends might cost us relationships. Would you rather do the wrong thing and get away with it, or do the right thing even if it might cost you? Are you willing to accept the cost of speaking the truth and saying no to the pressures of others? It's hard to do the right thing, especially when you see people doing wrong and getting ahead. Psalm 37:7

says, "Be still before the Lord and wait patiently for the Lord. Don't worry about evil people who prosper." When people do wrong it eventually catches up with them. Even if they do not get caught, their actions damage their character. It is hard to resist the pressures of others, but Joseph decided that having a good character was better than getting ahead by doing wrong. Character is worth more than popularity, money, or power. Do what's right and wait patiently for the Lord. You will see that it always pays off in the end.

Affirmation: I will not be pressured to do the wrong thing.
Prayer: Give me the strength to choose good character over getting ahead.

Day 16 - Adversity

Sometimes it can feel like you can't catch a break. Life just does not always go the way we plan. Indeed, there's one thing you can count on in life: you will face adversity. Adversity means hardship, difficulty, and challenges, and adversity is also what produces character. Adversity is what makes us grow. Martin Luther King, Jr. said, "The ultimate measure of a man (or woman), is not where they stand in moments of comfort and convenience, but where they stand in times of challenge and controversy." Joseph faces challenge after challenge. He is sold by his brothers into slavery, faced with sexual temptation, and thrown into prison for a crime he didn't commit. When Joseph finds himself in a situation he didn't choose, how does he handle this adversity? He does not quit or give in to self-pity. He also does not blame anyone else nor does he curse God. He takes the cards he is dealt and sees what he can do with them. He sees where he can use his gifts and become a stronger leader in whatever situation he is in. He has faith that God will bring him through whatever adversity he faces. Faith does not mean we will avoid suffering and adversity, but that we trust God to bring redemption out of it.

Affirmation: The adversity in my life is making me a stronger leader.
Prayer: Bring redemption out of my suffering, dear God.

Day 17 - Integrity

Integrity means living out what we say we believe. It's "who we are when nobody's looking." Integrity is being honest and truthful. It is the internal code we live by. We all have a set of standards that we choose to live by. When we do not live up to these standards we feel disconnected from ourselves.

When I was growing up I was one person at church and a different person at school. I became what the Bible calls "double-minded." It was like having my feet in two different canoes as I felt like I was being pulled in two different directions. Finally, I had to choose which person I was going to be. Integrity is being single-minded. This means we are the same person no matter where we are. I started bringing my faith side to school and inviting my school friends to church. I became part of Fellowship of Christian Athletes at school, which helped me "come out" as a Christian. We organized prayer before school around the flagpole. It felt so good to be the same person at school and church rather than two different people. Do you bring your faith side to school and work, or do you leave it at church on Sundays? Who are you when no one's looking? How do you want to practice integrity in your life?

Affirmation: I can live a life of integrity.
Prayer: Lord, help me have integrity even when no one is looking.

Day 18 - Fruit of Suffering

Joseph named his firstborn son Ephraim, which means: fruit of suffering. At the end of Joseph's long adversity, he is able to look back and see positive fruit that came out of his suffering. Have you experienced this? Have you gone through something hard that has caused you pain and suffering, but you came away stronger, better, or wiser? This is what redemption is and this is what God loves to do. God is able to bring good out of the worst situations. God does not cause our suffering, but God can use all our experiences to make us stronger, better, and wiser. The apostle Paul wrote in Romans 5:3, "We also glory in our sufferings, because suffering produces perseverance; perseverance produces character; and character produces hope." This is the fruit of suffering and it gives me hope. God is able to bring about good even in life's toughest moments. Maybe you are going through a struggle right now. What is the fruit of your suffering?

Affirmation: I am being made stronger, better, and wiser through my suffering.
Prayer: God, give me hope in the midst of my struggles.

Day 19 - Forgetting Trouble

Joseph had a second son named Manasseh, which means, "forgetting trouble." I used to have a strategy for getting through painful moments, whether it was enduring a painful drilling at the dentist or recovering from a sports injury. It even worked when I had a really bad outbreak of acne. I would simply remind myself that no matter how bad I might feel in the moment, it was only temporary. It would pass, the pain will end, the body will heal, and the embarrassment will fade. Pain stinks, but it does not last forever. Because the end of Joseph's life was so good, he forgot all about the trouble he experienced in his earlier days. His experience gave him new perspective on his pain. That's what we need: perspective on our pain. If all we focus on is how bad it seems right now in the moment, we will be miserable, but if we can remember that the pain is temporary, we can have peace even in the midst of life's storms. This is what the Psalmist meant when he said, "Weeping may endure for a night, but joy comes in the morning" Psalms 30:5. One of the final promises in Revelation is that God will wipe away every tear from our eyes. "There will be no more death or mourning or crying or pain, for the old order of things has passed away" Rev. 21:4. That's something to remember when we are going through trouble down here. When God's kingdom comes, our trouble will be completely forgotten.

Affirmation: All my pain and trouble will be forgotten.
Prayer: Lord, help me remember my pain is only temporary, and that joy comes in the morning.

Day 20 - Leadership Lessons: Problem-solving

"Houston, we have a problem." Jim Lovell uttered these words when an oxygen tank exploded on the Apollo 13 space shuttle in 1970, leaving the lives of three astronauts in peril. The NASA astronauts in space and engineers on the ground in Houston, Texas had to come up with a solution to fix the spacecraft that was 200,000 miles in space. With a limited amount of material, including some rolls of duct tape, they were able to fix the problem and make it safely back to earth. In life, you are faced with difficult situations like these. Sometimes you are dealt a bad hand. This is the test of leadership. What do you do when faced with this kind of situation? Do you give up? Or do you make the most of the situation? If the astronauts and engineers had given up it would have cost the lives of the whole crew. For them, failure was not an option. They took what they had to work with and came up with a solution. Joseph is dealt a bad hand. As bad things keep happening to him, he could have easily given up. The tragedy could have been the end of his story. Instead, it was just a chapter. Joseph used what he had available, and used his gifts to bring value to others. He was patient but stepped up when the opportunities came up. As a result, Joseph became a great leader who ended up saving the lives of many, including his family, during a great famine.

Affirmation: I am a leader.
Prayer: God, help me use what I've been given to become the best leader I can be.

Day 21 - Setting Prisoners Free

Every Saturday morning, youth from the west side of Chicago are provided a safe place to reflect, create, and express themselves through music. Started as a ministry of support for children and families with incarcerated loved ones, it has become a secondary family for many. One Saturday Tyrese*, a seven-year-old student in our drum line, was asked, "What was your best vacation and what made it so good?" As he paused to speak, I became very curious as to what he might say. Disney World? The Grand Canyon? My internal quandary was interrupted when Tyrese shouted out, "When I visited my dad in prison, because I have fun with my dad!" After Tyrese spoke, there was a brief moment of sacred silence in the room. For me, it was a reminder that underneath the tough facades, many youth are experiencing pain and loneliness. Regardless of the guilt or innocence of those incarcerated, it is the innocent children and families that are forced to pay the heaviest price. The truth is, the prison system is a destructive and violent force in the lives of children and families in our community. America has more people in prison than any other country in the world. In the same way it was not right that Joseph was falsely arrested, it is not right or just that Tyrese's best vacation is visiting a prison. But I have hope because Jesus came to "set the prisoners free" Luke 4:18. That is how I know Jesus is on Tyrese's side.

Affirmation: I am free in Christ.
Prayer: Jesus, help prisoners and their families know Your freedom and love.

Day 22 - Valuing Self, Valuing Others

To value others you have to first learn to value yourself. Jesus said the greatest commandment is to "love God with all your heart, mind, soul, and strength, and to love your neighbor as yourself" Luke 10:27. To love others like you love yourself requires you to love yourself. Jesus wants us to treat others like we would want to be treated. We have to learn to treat ourselves well and love ourselves so that we know how to show that love to others. I have seen people trying to love others while hating themselves. This will only work for a while. Eventually, you will resent the people you love. For those who try to love others while neglecting themselves they may need to turn the commandment around. You might have to read it as love yourself as you love your neighbor. Either way, it works. We are to have the same love for neighbor as we do for ourselves. Value yourself so you can value others; say kind words to yourself like you say kind words to others; encourage yourself in your talents like you encourage others. As you show love to yourself you will find you will be able to better love others.

Affirmation: These are three things I love about myself: 1._____ 2._____ 3._____
Prayer: Lord, help me to love myself as I love others.

Day 23 - Don't Stop Believing

I wonder if Joseph ever doubted God. I wonder if he ever lost faith. I think he probably did. You know why? Because we all do. Even Mother Teresa did. After she died, her private letters were published. In those letters, she expressed many moments of feeling far from God; and there were times she lost faith and experienced depression. People were shocked to read that someone as godly as Mother Teresa also had times of doubt and discouragement. But what is amazing is, even though she went through long spells of darkness and depression, she never stop serving God and loving people. Somewhere we got the idea that to have faith means to never doubt. That's not what faith is all about. Faith means trusting even when you experience doubt, fear, and darkness. Faith is a choice to believe, not a feeling. We have to choose to keep on believing. "Cling to your faith in Christ, and keep your conscience clear" 1 Timothy 1:19.

Affirmation: I won't stop believing.
Prayer: Dear God, help my doubts and questions lead me to deeper faith and truth.

Day 24 - You Can Do It!

In almost every Adam Sandler movie Rob Schneider appears, always as a different character, to yell out "You can do it!" It's a humorous but inspirational reminder to the main character that he can accomplish what he sets out to do. One of my favorite verses growing up was Philippians 4:13: "I can do all things through Christ who strengthens me." Reflecting on that big promise, I used to wonder if there were any limits to that passage. Does it mean I can lift a car off the ground? I don't think that's what it means, although I have heard stories where a mom actually lifted a car off the ground when her baby was stuck underneath. But I think it means something different. I think it means this: with Christ's strength I can endure any situation life throws at me. There will never be a situation I face where I cannot overcome it with Christ's help. When we cry out for help, God answers. When we face giants, we have the power of God at our back. When we find ourselves in prisons, the Lord is there with us. Instead of being intimidated or afraid, remember Christ is with you. If you listen closely, you may just hear him say to you, "You can do it!"

Affirmation: I can do all things through Christ who strengthens me.
Prayer: Lord, give me the strength to overcome any challenge I face today.

Day 25 - Greater Works

Jesus said to his disciples, "Even greater works than this will you do" John 14:12. This is hard to believe. Jesus is telling us that we have the potential to do even greater things than He did. Jesus did some pretty great things: He healed the blind, He walked on water, and He confronted those who exploited the poor and weak. Last time I checked I have not done any miracles. How are we to do greater things? Well, I have a theory. When Jesus became a man he was limited and could only be in one physical place at a time. The reason the disciples could do greater things is because they were more than one person so they were able to multiply the work Jesus' was able to do. This was Jesus' strategy all along. Jesus was not just trying to do ministry while he was on earth. He was pouring into the disciples so they could do it. Jesus envisioned them pouring into others who would in turn pour into others. When you think of it like this, it's pretty incredible. You and I are followers of Christ because of a long line of disciples who passed along Jesus message. It's like the game telephone but with billions of people over the span of two thousand years! Because Jesus taught the disciples how to love God, love people, serve the poor, and pray for their enemies, the disciples were able to make an impact for generations and generations. There are a billion people who profess to be Christians who can spread the love of Christ to the world. I wasn't the best in math, but I know a billion people are greater than just one person. Because Jesus ascended to Heaven, he was able to send his spirit into our hearts so that we could continue his ministry. We are able to do greater works when we allow the Spirit of Jesus to work through us to meet the needs of the world.

Affirmation: I can do even greater works.
Prayer: Lord, help me to spread your love to more people in more places.

Day 26 - Flip the Script

God loves to flip the script. When things seem hopeless God loves to step in and turn things around. Joseph's future looked bleak. When his chances of freedom didn't look good, God flipped the script. Pharaoh had a troubling dream that no one else could figure out and Joseph was able to interpret it and earn his freedom. Joseph could not have seen that coming; it must have at first seemed like evil would prevail and all hope seemed lost. But, then God flipped the script. Similarly, Daniel was given a death sentence but then remarkably he was rescued from a lion's den without a scratch. And, the disciples' hopes were crushed when Jesus was beaten violently and nailed to a cross, but three days later Christ was raised to life. God flipped the script! What are the obstacles you face? What are the disadvantages holding you back? God wants to flip the script. God often works when all hope seems lost. The evil that you and I experience is not the end of the story. God is always at work. God wants to flip the script in your life.

Affirmation: God has a plan for my life.
Prayer: God, flip the script in my life so I can encourage others who feel hopeless.

Day 27 - Sweet Revenge

If you really think about it, the plot to every action movie is revenge. There's typically a good guy who is getting back at a bad guy for doing something wrong. The climax of the movie is when the good guy finally gets even with the bad guy. One of my favorite movies is *The Count of Monte Cristo*. The main character is falsely accused and imprisoned after his best friend betrays him. During his time in prison he plots an elaborate escape to seek revenge. After years of struggle he finally gets retribution. I have to admit it's pretty satisfying when he finally gets even. I guess that's why they call it "sweet revenge." There's something in us that likes to see someone pay for his or her crimes. Perhaps we have been conditioned by watching too many action movies, or maybe it's just how we are wired as human beings. We want people to pay for what they do to us. That's why we lock people up and sentence them to death. But this is very different from the heart of God. We want retribution, but God wants restitution. We want an "eye for an eye," but God wants us to love our enemies. We want retaliation, while God wants reconciliation. Joseph naturally wanted revenge on his brothers and had the opportunity to make them pay. He could have denied them grain during a famine; they were at his mercy and he wanted to see them suffer. But in the end, he chose not to return hatred for hatred, but rather to "overcome evil with good" 1 Peter 3:9. The Bible says, "Vengeance is the Lord's" Deut. 32:35, so we should stop trying to enact revenge on others and let God be the judge.

Affirmation: I choose reconciliation over revenge.
Prayer: God, I will let You be the judge.

Day 28 - An Eye for an Eye

Gandhi said, "An eye for an eye leaves the whole world blind." When we return hatred for hatred, we might feel better but we have not really made things better. We have really only multiplied hatred in the world. The problem with hatred and violence is that it never ends. You kill my friend so I kill your friend. I kill your friend so you kill my brother. You kill my brother so I kill your mother. And on and on it goes; it is a never-ending cycle. That's why there were family feuds that went on for generations. That's why there are countries that are always at war. If we keep taking an eye for an eye we will all end up blind. Someone has to stop the cycle. Jesus taught us the way to break the cycle is to love our enemies and pray for those who persecute us, but this is hard to do; it takes real courage. When we do not return evil for evil, we plant seeds of goodness in the world; and when we love our enemies we multiply love and peace instead of multiplying hatred and violence. By ending the cycles of violence we end up changing the world.

Affirmation: I can change the world.
Prayer: Lord, help me love my enemies.

Day 29 - Anger

I had a lot of anger growing up and didn't know how to express it in healthy ways. I would get so mad I would punch walls until my knuckles would bleed. I grew up thinking anger was bad so I tried to squash it, but it would eventually come out. But it is not a sin to be angry. The Bible says, "In your anger, do not sin" Eph. 4:26. Feeling anger is natural and normal. In fact, if you never feel angry, I might be more worried. Joseph wrestled with anger toward his family. Joseph's anger presented him with a choice. He could continue to let his anger eat away at him, or he could express the sadness and hurt and seek forgiveness. He chose the latter, and it brought healing to him and his family. You are going to get angry and it isn't a sign of defect. Jesus got angry when he saw injustice. Remember when he overthrew the moneychangers who exploited people outside the temple? (Matt. 21:12) There's a place for anger when it's directed toward injustice. There are things we should get angry about. We should be angry about abuse, exploitation, sexism, and racism. Our challenge is to not sin in our anger. We can express our sadness, disappointment, and disapproval without causing injury to another. Anger helps us know what bothers us so we can address the deeper issues.

Affirmation: I can express my anger in healthy ways.
Prayer: Lord, help me to not sin in my anger.

Day 30 - Forgiveness

The hardest thing I have ever had to do was forgive. It's hard to let go of anger and pain. Joseph was so angry with his brothers and he didn't want to let them off the hook. They caused so much emotional anguish and unnecessary suffering in his life. Though he was justified to hate his brothers, Joseph chose to forgive them. Forgiveness frees us from hatred. When we don't forgive, we hold the hatred inside and it ends up hurting us more than it hurts the object of our hatred. When we hold anger inside, we end up damaging ourselves. It's been said; holding onto anger is like swallowing poison and expecting the other person to die. The way to freedom from anger, hatred, and resentment is forgiveness. Forgiving someone does not mean what they did was right; it also does not mean we have to keep spending time with them if they continue their behavior. It simply means we will no longer hold onto the hurt they have caused. Forgiving is good for our own soul as well as for the other person's soul. When I have chosen the hard path of forgiveness, it has helped me lay down the burden of anger and resentment. It has allowed me to be free.

Affirmation: I will forgive to free myself from hatred.
Prayer: Lord, lead me to a place of forgiveness so I can be free.

BONUS Day 31 - Never, Ever Give In

Winston Churchill, the Prime Minister of Great Britain during World War II, gave a famous speech at the school he attended as a youth. Near the end of the speech he exhorted the students with these famous lines: "Never give in. Never, give in. Never, never, never, never—in nothing, great or small, large or petty—never give in, except to convictions of honor and good sense. Never yield to force. Never yield to the apparently overwhelming might of the enemy." Love, peace, and goodness can never give in to hatred, violence, and evil. If good gives up then evil wins. As Edmund Burke so eloquently said, "All that is necessary for the triumph of evil is that good men (and women) do nothing." We cannot give up in the face of cynicism and evil. Hope is one of the most powerful forces in the world. Hope is contagious. When we start to hope then others have hope as well. We all face dark moments. That is when hope is needed most. Hope rebuilds after a hurricane sweeps through our city or a shooting happens in our community. Whatever struggle you are going through, don't give in to despair. Don't give in to fear. Never give in.

Affirmation: I will never give in to fear and despair.
Prayer: Lord, give me hope so I can give hope to others.

BONUS Day 32 - God Is in Control

A popular saying now is, "everything happens for a reason." I think people say this to feel more in control of their lives. It has a ring of truth to it. Though it may make us feel better about what we are going through, but I'm just not sure it's true. From Joseph's story, I see that human beings have a choice. His brothers chose to do evil to Joseph. Potiphar's wife chose to lie. But there's a difference between everything happening for a reason and God bringing good out of bad situations. When we say everything happens for a reason, we end up implying God approves all the bad things that happen to us. I do not think God causes the bad things that happen to us, but God does take the bad things that happen and bring good from them. See the difference? Joseph said to his brothers, "What you meant for evil, God meant for good" Gen. 50:20. Everything may not happen for a reason, but God is able to work goodness into the midst of evil when we put our lives in His hands. "And we know that in all things God works for the good of those who love Him, who have been called according to His purpose" Rom. 8:28.

Affirmation: My life is in Your hands.
Prayer: Lord, work all things together for Your good purposes.

CHAPTER EIGHT
- THE BOY WITH AN EVIL SPIRIT -

KEVIN ALTON

Day 1 - Desperate Hope

Sometimes we'll try anything.

The father in Mark 9 hadn't just spent the afternoon trying to figure out how to help his son; this had been a lifelong pursuit. It's almost surprising that the man even bothered to come to Jesus. I don't think that anyone would have blamed this dad for long ago giving up on finding a cure for his son and simply settling for trying to protect the son from himself.

If you've not experienced it yourself, there's no real way to describe what it feels like to be at that ragged edge of desperation, simultaneously clinging to and losing hope. It's as though each new thing that doesn't resolve the problem loosens your grip on believing that things can change.

The phrase "desperate hope" is an oxymoron that sums up the feeling well. The definition of desperate actually includes the characteristic of hopelessness. But "hopeless hope" is where God will meet us time and time again.

This doesn't mean that everything will work out like you want it to every time if you just believe hard enough or pray in the right way; there are times that we learn more about our own character or about the love of God when things *don't* turn out like we'd hoped. But, the love of God is unending, and in that concept, there is always hope.

Affirmation: My hope in God is well founded; there is no greater source.
Prayer: God, may my hope always remain in You; help me to trust and find peace in You.

Day 2 - Fighting a Losing Battle

There's a big difference between not giving up hope and picking a fight that you can't win. Many of today's "demons" are self-inflicted—drugs, alcohol, and other forms of addiction can change who people are. Romal describes the way addiction can affect people, even making them unrecognizable; the addict is suddenly no longer the person you once knew. Complicating things even further, which means that anything you might once have been able to say or do to help him won't help this person that he has become!

My younger brother has been diabetic for most of his life. When you have diabetes, your blood sugar can shift violently from highs to lows, or the other way around. While growing up, we shared a room and I can remember several middle-of-the-night episodes of him waking in a convulsing, out-of-control diabetic reaction. I'd leap from my bunk and yell for my parents. Together we'd physically drag him to the kitchen where we'd force glucose and orange juice down his throat while he would be thrashing, fighting us, and at times swearing like a sailor. My brother wasn't himself during those episodes; he had no idea where he was, and he wasn't consciously aware of us.

It was terrifying for me as a kid and I can't imagine what my parents were experiencing. This was something that was beyond our control. With modern medicine and the advice of doctors, we were able to help him learn to manage his diabetes as he got older.

The father in Mark 9 had no such reassurance. Without Jesus, fighting his son's condition wouldn't have been possible.

Affirmation: There are many things that I can overcome on my own, but it is a natural and healthy thing to admit when I need help.
Prayer: God, please show me when I'm fighting "demons" that are beyond my ability to conquer in life.

Day 3 - Loving for the Sake of Loving

In just a few months I'll have been a parent for ten years. I still don't have any idea what I'm doing.

There is some cumulative knowledge that you gather along the way that helps you keep your kids alive and dressed more or less in the way they'd like to be, but each new problem they face in life or circumstance that they don't understand is often as foreign to me as it is to my boys.

I can distinctly remember, though, a few instances that have really shaped how I approach problem solving with my kids. Obviously many "kid problems" aren't problems for adults at all, and we often have the tendency to fire off a solution at them with a tone that's less than gracious. "Find another pair of shoes," is a common response to one of our sons when he's holding a shoe for which he can't find the match. But one day, after a similar parental response, I remember being frozen by my son's facial expression when I instantly flashed back to my own childhood; my son's face mirrored a feeling deep in my past of not *being understood*. The shoes didn't matter; instead, what mattered was that my son felt heard.

When those around us are fighting to overcome addictions or behaviors or circumstances, they may not need anyone to yell the answers to them, though answers are often helpful. What they need *first* is to know that they are loved. They need to feel heard.

Affirmation: I can show God's love to those around me by listening more deeply than I speak.
Prayer: God, open my ears before putting words in my mouth. Help me to show Your love to those around me.

Day 4 - Have a Little Talk with Jesus

As a youth minister, I spend a lot of time saying, "If you ever need anything . . ." and "If you ever want to talk about . . ." And yet, there's an odd thing about church people. They don't like to ask for help when the water of life is waist deep; instead, they seem to prefer to wait until it is neck deep -- or until someone has already gone under -- before reaching out for help.

When the dam finally breaks (I think we can wrap up that metaphor now) and they finally sit down or ask me over to the house for "the conversation," the end of that time together usually concludes with deep gratitude. But, alongside the gratitude, hey often offer an apology to me, either about "taking my time" or about "bothering me with all of this." My response is always the same: "*This* is why I do this job."

God is more than equally available to you or anyone you may know in times of trouble. How long do you think the man waited to bring his son to Jesus in Mark 9? Can you hear the "Hey, I don't want to bug you, but..." in his "if you can do anything" request? Draw near to God and God will draw near to you. Even better—be in the practice of drawing near to God even when you don't need something. It's always easier to ask for help when you're already in relationship with someone.

Affirmation: Jesus is always waiting to hear from me.
Prayer: God, let me feel washed in your love and acceptance of me. Don't let me hesitate to come to You with all of my joys, sorrows, and struggles.

Day 5 - The Blame Game

While I was still a volunteer in youth ministry, I was on a fall retreat at Camp Lookout on Lookout Mountain just outside of Chattanooga, Tennessee. Our group was participating in some team-building exercises: climbing walls, getting through the rope course, navigating trust falls, and so on. We'd moved to the nearby woods for a final exercise that involved three platforms and a single two by eight just long enough to reach from one platform to the next.

The idea was to get the entire group on the first platform and then move all of them from the second to the third without anything touching the ground, using only the two by eight and whatever plans their hive-minded creativity could generate. It went great for a while; they very nearly did it in one try. Everyone was cheering the individual successes. But, with two people left to move from the second platform to the third, somebody stopped paying attention for a moment and the end of the two by eight hit the ground. The plan had been fine; a lapse in focus meant they'd have to start over.

Uproar. We heard things like: "*You* dropped it!" "It was *your* job to stand on it!" "He should have been helping!" In the midst of the arguing, while suppressing a laugh, our leader Patrick yelled out, "Yes! Quickly, assign blame!"

It's a go-to phrase I've carried with me since then. I bring it out any time a process, conversation or problem-solving effort gets bogged down in the question of who-did-what to cause the last effort to fail, instead of thinking of what might be helpful *next* time.

It's just as true when you're trying to restore a loved one to wholeness from addiction or harmful behaviors; even accurately assigning blame does nothing to advance healing.

Affirmation: I should be looking for what the next best thing is in all situations.
Prayer: God, keep my mind from busying itself with unhelpful negativity.

Day 6 - Home Alone

While I was growing up, I was almost never alone. My mom didn't have to work while we were little, and even when we got older; there was generally a parent in the house. This was not because my parents didn't trust us kids; it was just rare that they both would be gone very often.

When I was in the sixth grade I made friends with the kid who lived next door, who was growing up in an equally loving home, but his parents both worked. My new friend also had a cable slide running down through the woods in his backyard, a .22 rifle, and access to firecrackers, HBO, and throwing stars. There was even a beer fridge in the basement.

Somehow, I managed to not fall in with all that my neighbor had to offer, though we did spend a good bit of time blowing up anthills with firecrackers. We both knew kids in our neighborhood who didn't have it as good as we did -- some kids, for example, on our school bus were neglected or even abused.

What do you do when you encounter someone in those circumstances? Are *you* in those circumstances?

Affirmation: I am strong enough to be God's person in this world, even if those I associate or live with those who struggle to do so.
Prayer: God, may I help others where I can and seek help of my own when I need it.

Day 7 - God Is Everywhere

Christians have a terrible habit: they invite people to church. I suppose it's fine to invite people to church. The "terrible habit" part comes in when we think that's the best way to invite them to *God*. That's what we're supposed to be there for.

We have a neighbor who lives across the street who is godlier than I am probably six days out of seven every week, if only in terms of the way she cares for her daughter. She's a single mom who works hard hours at a physical job. She gets up early and goes to bed earlier. She watches our kids for free sometimes so that my wife and I can go on dates. Her daughter comes with our boys to church sometimes, but they don't have any routine practice of attending church.

One Sunday, I can remember coming home from church after a particularly engaging sermon about living as servants to those around us as a way to share the love of God in our community. The day before, I had spent the afternoon cutting down and chopping up two dead trees in our front yard. I left all of the logs and branches lying there, figuring to get to them the next week sometime. As we pulled up the driveway, my wife noticed that the mess from the chopped down trees was completely gone. How did that happen, we wondered? We found out that our neighbor across the street, the single mom, "had an extra hour" and cleaned it up for us.

God's love changes people; they don't have to be in a church for that to happen. God's love seeps out of our neighbor. God's love found Romal's mom right where she was. God's love can find you.

Affirmation: I am loved by God and I have the ability to pass that love on to others.
Prayer: God, let others see your love beyond the church in *who I am in You.*

Day 8 - Falling in Love with You

One of the biggest hurdles that Romal's mom faced on her road to recovery was rebuilding her ability to love herself. She had done things to herself, her family, and her son that were hard for others to forgive; they had to be even harder for her to overcome.

I've struggled my whole life with depression. Unfortunately, for years I didn't realize that I was struggling with depression. Decades, even. By that time I was engaging in behaviors and thoughts that were either already harming me or were capable of doing so soon.

A few years ago, with the help of my loving life partner, I slowly began to rebuild who I would allow myself to be. For all of those years, I'd been pushing away my own potential. In my own mind, I didn't hold any real value. Why would anything good come from me? Why should anyone love me?

In re-learning to love myself, a fascinating thing happened: I re-learned how to love others. And, I re-learned how to love God.

Affirmation: I can love me. There are things about me that I may still be learning to love, but I am lovable.
Prayer: God, show me Your love in a way that allows me to love myself as well.

Day 9 - Mad at God

Imagine how much less inspiring the story about the possessed young man would be if, in the next few verses after Jesus healed him, a bear ate him in front of his family. We like our stories to go a certain way, don't we? We expect the good guy to win and look for "happy ever after," and so on. But, we know real life isn't like that. That kid *did* die at some point, but it's a likeable story because the story ends right in the middle of the good part. Romal's story about his mom could have had a nice rosy finish, too, if he had stopped telling it as her life turned around and she came to know God. But Romal didn't stop sharing, because life kept going. His mom got cancer, and he'd lost her more quickly than he'd gotten her back.

My own mother died right in the middle of a good part of her story, too. When I was in high school, my mom, in her forties, went to college. She was an incredibly popular substitute teacher and felt that God was calling her to a new career in education after having been a homemaker throughout our childhood.

And she nearly did it. In the year that she would have graduated from college, we found out she had cancer. I can still remember her in tears, adamant that this wasn't going to be the end of her; she reasoned that God wouldn't have brought her this far only to let her die. She died six months later.

I don't really remember being mad at God, but the people in the church culture I grew up in believed deeply that everything happened for a reason, and that everything was part of God's plan, which I found confusing to say the least. God's plan was for mom to die right then? God had a *reason* for that?

It wasn't until I was an adult that I saw a kind of beauty in the timing of my mother's death —she died pursuing something she believed God was calling her toward. How else would anyone want to go?

Affirmation: Life brings great sorrow at times, but I can find peace with God.
Prayer: God, keep my head above water and help me not be overcome by the sorrows of this world.

Day 10 - Falling Down

We live in a farmhouse built in the 1930s.

No, not the scenic one you're picturing, the other kind. It was a simply-built, four-room structure with no bathroom. It was crafted from wood milled from the trees cleared to make room for it. The supporting band of the house is actually made of whole *tree* sections, tops and bottoms planed flat to allow for an even construction surface. Rocks found on the property support the whole thing.

Our house has a lot of character. Someone added a bathroom, and, from what we can tell, in the 1960s, they added a living room to one side, resulting in the two-bedroom, one-bath home we now reside in with our two boys. When we had it inspected before buying it, we were told that it would have to be completely rewired if we didn't want it to burn down, a repair accommodated before closing. Before we decided to buy it, we were standing in the kitchen with the inspector next to a spot that was visibly out of level. Was that a problem?

"The whole house is out of level," the inspector said. "But it's been settling for eighty years. If you look at it like that, it's not really going anywhere."

We don't know how it got out of level and it must have taken a long time to get that way. The father of the boy in Mark 9 probably couldn't have told you the day they noticed something was wrong with his son; at this point it was just "since childhood." And, addiction and harmful behaviors similarly develop over time.

Affirmation: I can give others and myself the time we need to heal from our hurt.
Prayer: God, thank You for your eternal patience and provision. Help me heal.

Day 11 - Never Give Up

When my family moved from our last church to our current church, the housing market was collapsing. It hadn't hit bottom yet, but it had clearly tumbled off of the cliff. When we put our house on the market, things weren't completely bleak, but our listing agent was a friend and was straightforward with us, saying: "This is going to be tough. No one is buying houses, especially not houses in your price range." He had at one point been our next-door neighbor, and confessed that when he sold his house, he took a significant loss.

So our house sat. And sat. Months went by without as much as a nibble. We were beginning to consider what it might look like if I had to commute to the new church from our house if it didn't sell. The idea of driving over an hour to an unknown community and trying to build relationships there wasn't appealing, and my delightful relic of an automobile wasn't likely to hold up to that kind of commute anyway.

On the other end of the journey, we weren't having a lot of success finding a house in our price range that we liked. There were plenty of fixer-uppers or really nice homes that we couldn't afford.

With just a couple of weeks until the start date for my new church position, both problems resolved simultaneously. We found the old farmhouse I talked about in yesterday's devotion, perfectly situated on land surrounded by forty acres of woods. They're not our woods, but we get to live near them. And our house sold. The buyers paid our asking price, and split the closing costs.

In the parking lot after closing on our house, our agent/friend looked me in the eye and said, "Dude. There is no way that your house just sold. I don't even mean the part about you getting your asking price. Only one comparable property has sold in our region in the last three months."

Sure, we could have given up and sold our house for less, and we could have given up and stayed where we were. But we didn't give up.

What if the father of this boy in Mark 9 had given up? What would have happened to the boy? If you were that father, how long would you keep looking for a cure for your son before giving up?

Affirmation: I will face adversity. Not giving up doesn't assure victory, but hanging in there builds my character and deepens my faith.
Prayer: God, I want to give up sometimes. When life seems too much, help me to keep trying.

Day 12 - God Can Take It

For most of our lives, we live through various social filters. We learn that in certain places with certain people, we're expected to behave one way, while in other circles we can be ourselves a little more freely.

When it comes to relationships where someone has authority over us, we learn to filter our opinions and emotions around them, especially if those opinions or emotions are about them. It's difficult, if not impossible, to really express anger at a boss or a parent without making the situation worse.

Because our view of God isn't perfect, very often we treat God like any other authority figure. We think that God has power, that he can make things happen that I can't, and he expects things of me. So, instead of viewing God as a mentor or a guide for discipleship, we turn God into an unquestionable "Boss of Me."

But, that's not fair to God or us. When we have doubts, fears, or even anger at or about God, where else can we go but to God? Is it wrong to throw all of that at God? Does being angry with God make us bad people or bad Christians?

I don't think so. Have you ever seen an angry child in the arms of a loving parent? The child squirms, wails, and flails his or her little arms while the parent waits for the tantrum to end; sometimes, the parent is even amused at the actions of the kid.

As we grow in our faith, like the child, we find new ways of expressing those doubts, fears, and anger. Our relationship with God matures, and we no longer need to throw the emotional fit.

Affirmation: God can handle any emotion I have or wish to express!
Prayer: God, help me remember that You created me as I am. Nothing I feel or think is a surprise to You.

Day 13 - People Will Let You Down

Romal describes the growing doubt of the father as a result of his experiences with other people, not his experience with God. How fast would your faith run out if it were based upon what you knew of other people?

I had wanted a motorcycle since I was a little kid. I think for me it was a progressive extension of wanting really cool bicycles—what could be cooler than a bicycle with a motor? For years, my wife was against the idea of the motorcycle, but at some point she relented. I found a little 1984 Honda Shadow that had been "customized," mostly meaning that the rear shocks and front and rear fenders had been removed. It looked kind of cool and lowered, and what that meant is it was a really hard ride. At one point, the rear tire actually ate through the wire to the taillight.

I bought the bike from a guy whom I only ever knew as "Rider." He bought old crappy bikes, fixed up the motors and repainted what needed repainting in a thrown together shop in his back yard. We became friends. Oddly enough, we never rode together, but we'd get together on the weekends and hang out at his house, tinkering on bikes or just sitting around talking.

About a year and a half after I'd met him, I dropped off my bike for an oil change. When I called a week later to arrange to pick it up, his wife answered the phone. I asked, "Is Rider there?" She said, "He's gone." I then asked, "When will he be back?" She repeated her answer, "No, I mean he's gone. He split. He was in trouble with some people and sold all the bikes in the shop for cash, then split."

The loss of my first motorcycle has rarely bothered me but the staggering betrayal of a friend has stayed with me. I don't think I was ever even angry with him, I just couldn't believe it. I never saw him again. Late one night, a couple of years later, he called, mumbling a drunken, incoherent apology. I wonder if he even knows he called.

I could have let that experience leak into other friendships; it would have been an easy thing to become distrustful, especially of meeting new people. The dad in our biblical story could equally have become distrustful of seeking help for his son; who knows what kinds of people or methods he put momentary faith in during his long journey of seeking help?

Affirmation: Community is a wonderful gift, but my deepest trust must be in God.
Prayer: God, I thank You for good friends and people that I can rely on. Help me to always rely most on You.

Day 14 - Might as Well Ask

When you go kayaking or canoeing, there's a little wrinkle that has to be worked out every time you go. If you intend to travel from point A to point B on the river, it's an unquestionable reality that the vehicle you intend to drive home can only be in one of those locations. The best solution is to go with friends in two vehicles; that way you can leave one car where you intend to exit the river and take the other one where you want to launch your boats.

But if you're going solo, it's trickier. During the summer months it's pretty easy to hitchhike between your put-in and takeout points. The paddling community is pretty laid back and looks out for each other. But during the winter months it's significantly harder to catch a ride. Fewer of the cars that are passing are paddlers, and non-paddlers aren't much into having your wet self in their car.

I developed an attitude similar to what the father in our story must have been feeling as he walked through life trying to find help for his son. I'd drop my boat at the put-in, drive my car to the takeout and start walking back; and, though I walked with my thumb out just in case, I had no real expectation that I'd be picked up. My odds did pick up slightly when it occurred to me to start wearing a sign reading, "Dry as a bone" on my back while walking, but most of the time I'd end up walking all the way back to my boat.

Imagine the father's similar grim resolve. Could Jesus help his son? The father might as well ask.

Affirmation: I don't have to wonder if Jesus can help me; God has proven time and time again that every moment in my life is surrounded with love and grace. **Prayer:** God, help me to reach through my doubts into the freedom of trusting You.

Day 15 - Trust and Obey

I'm leaving my church. Because God told me to.

I've been in youth ministry a long time; it was the oddest thing to wake up one morning realizing, "Kev, it's time to go." Until that moment, we'd had no inclination that our time at the church might be coming to an end; things were going well and we felt like we were right where we were supposed to be.

Romal talks about obedience to God as being one of the more difficult things we'll ever do. We like to be in charge; we don't want to let some other person or presence dictate what we'll do with our lives. For some reason, once you start being obedient to God with your life, it doesn't get easier. Continuing to be obedient is hard. We think to ourselves, "I already obeyed, God! Why can't you just leave me alone?"

Romal's mom had to make the difficult decision to obey God. While that initial obedience brought obvious benefits to her life, there were certainly additional things that she had to obey going forward that weren't as obviously beneficial; changes in relationships, motivation, and her attitude toward life all probably came into play.

For me, the call to obedience is to step out as a freelance writer and speaker about age-level ministry. "Freelance" doesn't come with a guaranteed paycheck. It's the most terrifying obeying we've ever done. But we're excited, because we trust God.

146

What does your next step of obedience need to be?

Affirmation: I am free to obey God with my goals and ambitions in life.
Prayer: God, sometimes I try to take control of everything; help me let go and learn to trust You more every day.

Day 16 - Relying on the Strength of Another

No path of recovery from drugs or other addictions is simple or easy. I don't know anyone who can remotely claim that he accomplished it on his own. Romal's mom's prayer perfectly states the vulnerability required in asking for help: "God, I'm not sure that I can do it, but I know you can. I know that I am weak, but you can give me the strength to beat this."

It's in our nature to be self-sufficient.

A few years ago I had to have back surgery. A little chunk of whatever it is between the sections of my spine was crushing my right sciatic nerve and had come out. I fought the pain for as long as I could, but one morning I couldn't even get out of bed.

For about two months, I had to rely on the strength of my wife Britta for nearly everything. I couldn't stand or sit without her help. Her patience had to have been tested; suddenly she was a single parent in charge of keeping house and waiting hand and foot on a six-foot-two inch dude on pain medication.

I never could have made it through that experience without my wife. She provided the strength that I didn't have on my own.

Affirmation: I don't have to do everything myself; there are many things I'm not even meant to do. God is my very present help in times of trouble (Psalm 46).
Prayer: God, help me swallow my pride and accept that I need You to help me; Your strength is greater than my own.

Day 17 - Finding the Root

We've talked about how it's okay to doubt and that God can handle your doubts, but Romal brings up an important step that a lot of people miss: discovering and confessing the source of our doubts.

For a few years I was a regular volunteer at a Native American nature preserve in Chattanooga. The biggest continual need was pulling up privet, a non-native plant that is aggressive undergrowth if left untended; it will kill off native plants by using the available nutrients in the soil. The Cherokee woman in charge of volunteer efforts emphasized that care must be taken not to simply snap the privet off at the level of the soil as it will simply grow back, often forming an even healthier plant. We were instructed to fully remove the privet plant – the root and all needed to be unearthed and discarded. The same is true of our doubts about God. If we don't take the time to dig in and discover the roots of those doubts, we may resolve them in the short term, but ultimately they'll come back every time.

Be patient. Dig deep. Find those roots.

Affirmation: It may take a while, but I'm willing to trace my doubts and fears about God to the source.
Prayer: God, I want to trust and believe in You fully! Help me discover where my doubts originate.

Day 18 - Seeing Is Believing

We could draw easy conclusions about the faith of the father in our story. We could presume he heard about Jesus somewhere; with his heart leaping with joy and belief, he raced to Jesus, son in tow, for the obvious happy ending.

That's not how we're wired though. Romal points out that the father's fullest moment of belief came in the experience of seeing the suffering of his son come to an end. Never again would he doubt the power of God.

When my oldest son Grey was about three years old, we were visiting friends who had a swimming pool. He always played on the steps and had proven to be relatively self-sufficient there as long as we kept an eye on him. But, on this day he slipped off the bottom step, instantly in over his head. His mom and I were both in the pool, about fifteen feet away. My instinct was to run toward him, which you cannot do in water. He'd been thrashing up and down enough to get air, and when his mom rescued him seconds later, he was absolutely terrified.

That fear stayed with my son for years. Even when all his friends were swimming and he was tall enough to walk around in the shallow end, he refused to let his head go below water. Even when we sent him to swimming lessons, there was no way he was he going to put his head underwater.

Then, we had a random breakthrough. We were at the community pool and I told Grey, "If you'll duck your head completely underwater, you can dunk me. You don't have to swim or jump in, just stand in place and squat enough that your head is completely underwater." Even that took a few hours, but he eventually did it, and the transformation was nearly instantaneously. Within a week he was letting high school kids throw him into the pool at a youth party.

Jesus did say that those who believe without seeing are blessed, but so often we're blessed by being shown.

Affirmation: If I keep my eyes open, God will show me great things.
Prayer: God, help me to believe without seeing when I can and to have the patience to wait to see what You choose to show me.

Day 19 - The Big Question

Could Jesus heal this boy?

Even though the story we're studying is very brief, there is a lot revealed about what has led up to this moment. The prolonged suffering of the boy, the tireless search for a cure by the father, and the witness of the community all come to bear in this moment. Can Jesus do it? *Will* Jesus do it?

Healing miracles are a nervous territory when it comes to faith in God. If healing doesn't come, what does that mean? Was God displeased for some reason? Did the person not have enough faith, or perhaps not ask in the right way? Is it a judgment by God?

There was a death of a beloved figure in our community. She was a teacher, mother, wife, friend, and devoted follower of Christ who beat cancer once, but it came back and her prognosis worsened at an accelerating pace. She was surrounded by praying friends nearly around the clock. The big question was: Would God heal her?

She never stopped believing that she would be healed, and therefore refused to make plans with friends and family for anything that might happen if she died. She didn't even talk to her kids about it. Anytime anyone suggested otherwise, she would always counter, "You still believe that I'm going to be healed, don't you?"

149

She's one of those wonderful people who is remembered more for how she lived than how she died, but the end was hard for everyone.

What do we do when "the big question" doesn't get the answer we wanted?

Affirmation: I must trust that God's thoughts are higher than mine; there will be things that happen in this life that I may never understand.
Prayer: God, help me to find Your peace and grace even in situations that I find disappointing.

Day 20 - Out of the Spotlight

I doubt that the father in our story would claim that he did anything extraordinary in coming to Jesus. Obviously this dad had given himself tirelessly over the course of the son's life, but that's hardly anything he'd probably want to take credit for.

It's a little like that quick human-interest story you see on the local half-hour newscast every few weeks, the one that they tease at the beginning of the show, but save for minute twenty-seven, just ahead of next week's weather forecast. The one about the driver that stopped to help the older lady out of an upended vehicle before authorities could arrive. Or, about the firefighter that went back into the burning building fourteen times to get all the kids, pets, and favorite books just before the house collapsed. When asked about their heroic actions, the heroes of these segments all seem to say roughly the same thing: "I just did what anybody would have done."

Just doing what anybody would have done didn't heal the boy in our story, but his father's effort put the kid in the presence of the one who was capable of being the superhero. The father could never claim that he accomplished it alone; without the actions of Jesus, it would just be one more unsuccessful attempt to help his son.

We're not superheroes either. We're not capable of lifting ourselves out of our own disasters. The more quickly we admit that, the more quickly we're on the road to finding the one who can help us—the one we'll be able to thank for the rest of our lives.

Affirmation: I can be saved from my present circumstances, but not by myself. I can trust God to do for me what I cannot do for myself.
Prayer: God, help me give place to Your overwhelming ability to heal and sustain me.

Day 21 - Putting in the Hours

Deciding to take the lead in the process of recovery from abuse or addiction is a monumental step, but it's just the first step.

Years ago my wife and I learned that friends of ours were on the verge of splitting up. It was one of those marriages where nobody saw it coming; everything looked fine from the outside. They had married young, and after nearly two decades and four kids things seemed pretty normal. I was better friends with the husband and I went to talk to him about it all one day.

Although it's a conversation that I've had more times than I care to count, this one was unique. There were not the usual one-sided accusations, but instead there was ownership of mistakes made along the way. As the conversation wrapped up, my friend said something that's stuck with me: "Everybody wants the quick answer about all of this. If we just said 'we're getting divorced' or 'we're fine now' everybody could just go back to worrying about their own lives, which is what they want to do. Nobody wants to let this thing take a little time, but the fact is, it's going to. We're trying. But we didn't get here overnight. It's going to take a while for things to heal, if they ever do."

That's a hard truth to recognize, and the implications can be intimidating when it comes to recovery. One day at a time is really what it's about.

Affirmation: Today is the only day I need to face today.
Prayer: God, whether in my own life or someone else's, let me be patient in times of healing.

Day 22 - Misplaced Anger

Romal talks about the sometimes-unpleasant transformation that can happen in a person as he or she works through recovery. It's a daily, sometimes hourly ordeal that can easily affect mood and disposition. The key is to remember that the person is not lashing out at you, he is just lashing out -- sometimes it's even directed at himself, even though it's coming out at you.

I had a situation within my first few months of leading the youth ministry at my current church that taught me this very lesson. There was a trip on our calendar that commanded a healthy chunk of our budget, and it was one of those situations where the cost of the trip didn't really go down or up much based on how many kids were going. If thirty were going, it felt like a worthwhile investment, but if only ten were going, it would start to feel like poor stewardship to go. We had three signed up on the last day we could cancel without a penalty. So, we decided to cancel and I sent an email to the parents with this information.

Later that night, I got a call from another staff member who encouraged me to check my email.

One of the parents in my youth program had blown up in an email, and I replied to the note. And, what was worse, I had accidentally hit the "reply all" button, so my searing response to the parent was sent to all in the original email thread. I had to call the parent to discuss the situation, and we were on the phone for an hour and half; the parent criticized my decision-making as well as my competency as a leader. I kept my composure with the parent, validating some of their thinking where I could, and we eventually called it a night, though still in disagreement.

Later I found out, it wasn't about me. I discovered that this parent was enduring some really difficult things at work and I was a safer target for letting off some steam than anyone at work. This parent later became one of my greatest supporters; but if I had responded in-kind during that first conversation, I might very well have been fired.

Affirmation: I need to try to control my own frustrations and allow others to express theirs without taking things personally.
Prayer: God, help me recognize when I'm hurting others with my hurts; help me extend grace to others who are doing the same.

Day 23 - Hands and Feet

When people first step into their journey of recovery, it's easy for others that have been trying to get them to that point to want to step back. "Thank God, our work is done." But Romal is quick to point out that's the moment that they really just begin to need you.

I need to confess a personal failure here to illustrate the point. Our church hosts a community-supported weekly recovery program. I've mentioned earlier that I live out in the country; there's nothing I could throw that would even make it out of the yard, let alone hit a neighbor's house. But there's a couple that lives nearby that fights so loudly that we can hear them inside our house. From inside *their* house. Sometimes it's in the yard. Sometimes they call the police on each other. It's a little crazy.

So one day, this couple drives up to our house, which was alarming. After working through a really awkward false premise for why they were there, it became clear that the real reason they were in my yard was that the husband wanted to know if our church's recovery program had anything for him, a man with anger issues. I said, "Absolutely!" and gave him the program times.

Good job, right?

No. Here a complete stranger exercises unbelievable vulnerability in my yard and my response is a very impersonal offering of information. What should I have done? I should have taken him in. Walked with him for a moment. That's what people in recovery need—company.

Affirmation: I can help somebody with something, even if I am in need of help myself.
Prayer: God, let me be Your hands and feet to someone in my life today.

Day 24 - Support, Love, and Encouragement

Healing from addiction is hard, as Romal shares regarding his mom's journey. A community of support is critical.

When my mom died, I had the terrific support of my church community. Many people said many things -- some of it helpful, some not -- and all comments were well intentioned, I'm sure.

One thing I'll never forget is the visit from my youth director. I wasn't surprised to see him; that's what youth ministers do when family members die. But after some general conversation, he asked me a question I've asked hundreds of youth since then: "Kevin, is your spiritual life in a place to handle this?"

That question did a number of things all at once. It told me that if I wasn't in a place to handle it, he was there to help. It made me take an honest look at my spiritual life, which is something we should probably all do more often anyway. And it made me realize with joy that I was more prepared spiritually to deal with my mom's death than I would have guessed.

I just needed a little support, love, and encouragement.

Affirmation: I am as much in need of love, support, and encouragement as I am in need of giving those things to others.
Prayer: God, help me to find the healing that comes from loving others.

Day 25 - Finding the Right Voices

As Romal's mom began to improve, they had to keep reminding her that she would have to stay focused on God, and that she would likely face resistance from anger and rejection.

Imagine the voices of discouragement and distraction that the dad in our story was facing while trying to help his son. Remember, he wasn't getting second opinions from different doctors. He was trying to get what he presumed was a demon out of his son. Most people probably believed there wasn't a fix for that.

Where do you turn to find the right voices? Friends? Mentors? Can you turn within to hear God's voice?

Affirmation: If I can slow down and still my spirit, I can hear the good voices over the bad.
Prayer: Thank You so much, God, for your continual voice of goodness in my spirit.

Day 26 - Knowing Your Limits

As we work alongside people in recovery, we can find ourselves inclined to take on more than we're capable of doing. If someone relapses, we feel like we've failed personally. We've got to realize that our desire to help doesn't translate directly to responsibility or even ability; remember the disciples asking, "Why couldn't *we* drive it out?"

Our youth group used to take an annual beach trip to Florida, but with the school's sport schedules increasingly choking out the kids' summers, we eventually had to let that one go.

On one of our last trips, we picked a bad week. It was nearly chilly, with a standing wind that made it less than pleasant to be outdoors. Worse, there was a severe riptide the whole time we were there; double red flags flew everywhere and they were patrolling the beach and actually shouting at anyone who wandered even ankle-deep in the water. Eleven people had died in the few days that we'd been there. Shockingly, most of the people who perished were attempting to save someone else. Heartbreaking.

When trying to help someone else, it's important to know your limitations.

Affirmation: My desire to help others is a godly response to those around me.
Prayer: God, allow me to help others to the extent that I am able.

Day 27 - Problem Solver

Instead of overstepping our roles as supporters, Romal encourages those of us who are loving others through recovery to stop trying to fix them and start trying to help them dream of a better future. Some people can't help others without taking over, but people who are recovering from addiction need to participate significantly in the process or they just won't learn anything.

When our boys were old enough to finally have actual homework when they came home from school, my wife and I evaluated how much we should assist them. On the one hand, we knew it was important to help explain any concepts or processes that they didn't quite understand from that day, but when it came down to the actual completion of their work, we were at a loss. Were we bad parents if we let them take a wrong answer to school the next day because they made a simple mistake? Or were we bad parents if we stood here and kept erasing wrong answers until they got them right?

As our children have gotten older we've found ways to set them up to fail productively. Or "give them chances to succeed" would probably be a better parenting term. But, we'll intentionally let them experience mistakes, because that's where you learn the most.

Where were you allowed the most freedom to succeed or fail on your own? What did you learn from those experiences?

Affirmation: I take pride in solving my own problems. I can encourage and support others, but whenever possible I should allow them to feel that kind of pride too.
Prayer: God, thank You for putting a helpful spirit within me and help me to know how to best use it.

Day 28 - Living the Dream

Dreams for the future are great; sharing your dreams for the life of someone near you that's recovering can help them form dreams of their own. You may be in the process of trying to free yourself from your past as well. Dreaming a new future can help focus the mind and push aside negative thinking.

But, Romal takes that concept a step further; as our dreams for the future begin to clarify, we must take those dreams to God in prayer.

For the past eleven months I've been praying about my new office. As soon as my wife and I accepted that God was calling us away from our current local church positions, we began casting visions—or dreaming—for what might be next. For my wife, we believe that she's going to be "Mom" for a while and support me as I launch into writing and speaking full time. Knowing that I would need a dedicated space for writing, I began to pray about "my new office." I would park outside of a possible space and pray over it. I wasn't trying to will it into being, but instead I was using it as a placeholder for a vision for the future. Eventually, I was dreaming of the furniture, art for the walls, even who might come visit me. Threaded through all of that was the vision for the work I believe God was calling me to create in this next part of my journey.

Bringing your dreams into your prayers is a powerful way to connect your inner self with God.

Affirmation: I am a dreamer!
Prayer: God, help my dreams for myself and others always focus on You.

Day 29 - The Ones You Love

I remember early on in discussion about taking on this project, I had sent an email to Romal expressing how deeply I'd felt his pain in the two preview chapters that I'd read. From having the strength to suffer the loss of a mother through childhood, to surviving the nerve-raw journey of recovery, to losing his mother just as his relationship with her was reforming, it was nearly too much to take as an outsider to his story.

Near the end of *God's Graffiti*, Romal reminds us to "never give up on the ones you love." It sounds like a simple statement, but the truth is that the million ways life comes at us can change whom we love and why. It would have been perfectly understandable for Romal to give up on his mom; she was more of a source of difficulty and pain through his childhood than anything you'd want or need from a mom.

What Romal actually lived out was not giving up on *love*. Thanks to God, he was able to set aside every natural inclination to leave all that his old life entailed behind him, and have faith that God could save his mom too, no matter what it took.

Affirmation: Love should be my first and last consideration in my interaction with everyone and anyone.
Prayer: Lord, I cannot begin to return to others the love that You have shown to me. Help me to try.

Day 30 - Doing What You Can

I think it's pretty clear that the father in Mark 9 didn't believe that he could help his son by himself. If he did, he'd have just stayed at home trying. But in Mark we find him creating a stir with scribes and disciples arguing, and Jesus intervening. The dad did what he could do and then got out of the way.

My little Georgia town was hit by a tornado in 2011. It's an unusual community among small town communities; it's one of those places where everybody still seems to know everybody and seems willing to lend a helping hand.

The tornado plowed right through the main street of town, wiping out restaurants and clipping two schools on its way out, including the stadium of our state-contending high school baseball. The storm hit in April, so repairs began in earnest in early summer.

I spoke that year with a friend who was the assistant principal (now principal) of that high school, commenting that it must have been a difficult summer. "Honestly, Kevin," he said, "this has been the easiest summer of my career. We're not even allowed at the school. The insurance company is handling everything. I've been at home or on the golf course."

I think our tendency to get in the way of the one most capable of resolving our problems is well-intentioned, but sometimes we need to just get out of the way and let God work.

Affirmation: If I'm willing to listen, God will reveal my role in every situation.
Prayer: God, show me where to jump in and help and—maybe more importantly—when to get out of the way!

CPSIA information can be obtained
at www.ICGtesting.com
Printed in the USA
FFOW05n1913201016

9 780990 591791